THINK AND TRADE LIKE A CHAMPION

The Secrets, Rules & Blunt Truths of a Stock Market Wizard

MARK MINERVINI

Access Publishing Group, LLC

ISBN 978-0-9963079-3-2 (pbk)

ISBN 978-0-9963079-4-9 (ebk)

Printed in the United States of America

Eleventh Printing

11

CONTENTS

FIRST STEPS TO THINKING AND TRADING LIKE A CHAMPION

You become what you think about all day long.

—*Ralph Waldo Emerson*

Think and Trade Like a Champion will help you take control of your trading by following timeless rules and proven techniques. You will receive answers to some of the toughest and most confusing questions, such as when to hold a short-term winner for a longer-term gain; when to cut your loss even before your stop is hit; how to establish the optimal position size; how and when to buy and sell; and exactly what to examine during post-trade analysis to improve your weaknesses and build a solid foundation for success.

In my first book, *Trade Like a Stock Market Wizard* (McGraw-Hill, 2013), I provided a foundation for those interested in learning my SEPA® trading strategy. While I never set out to write a two-volume set, this book contains many of the things I could not fit in the first book due to space limitation.

In the following pages, I divulge my personal recipe for trading success based on 33 years of experience and real-life application; this invaluable "how-to" on the strategy led me to become a U.S. Investing Champion and turn a few thousand dollars into a multimillion-dollar fortune.

You may not have three decades of experience like me, but you have something else that is very valuable, something that can shorten your learning curve dramatically: the opportunity to use my knowledge as your starting point. This means you have the opportunity to achieve even greater success than I have.

Now, maybe you're thinking, *Mark became a champion investor when trading was easier*, or, *Mark is naturally gifted or had an upbringing that gave him certain advantages*. Nothing could be further from the truth. I started out poor with little education or capital. When I began trading, commissions were hundreds of dollars per trade versus just $5 or $10 today. Bid and ask spreads were often $2 or $3 versus only pennies now. And most of all, there was little access to superior knowledge. Today you have direct access to everything you need—tools and knowledge that were once only available to elite Wall Street pros. It's a great time to pursue stock investing.

However, you should know that even the right knowledge, hard work, and practice will not necessarily get you any closer to trading success. People who work hard but practice the wrong things will only engrain bad habits and perfect faulty mechanics. In *Think and Trade Like a Champion*, you will learn the correct way to practice—exactly what to do and what to avoid.

I'm here to tell you that your own ability is far greater than your wildest imagination. I guarantee you are operating at only a fraction of your true potential. That's true in life, and it's certainly true for trading. Let me assure you, anyone can achieve superperformance in stocks if they set their mind to it. It requires the right knowledge, a commitment to the learning process, and the will to persist. It's not going to happen overnight, but with the right tools and the right attitude, you can do it.

DECIDE TO DECIDE

In the stock market and in life, we choose to win and we choose to lose. That's right! We lose because we want to lose, and we win when we decide that we're going to be winners. While this statement may strike you as incorrect or patently unfair, I know it to be true. In more than three decades as a full-time stock trader, I've witnessed people who lose because they want, consciously or unconsciously, to fail. And I've seen those who decided once and for all that they were going to be successful, and they transformed themselves from mediocre to extraordinary. Winning, without a doubt, is a choice!

If you don't accept this, then, by default, you must believe that you have no control over your destiny. And if that's true, then what's the point of even trying to succeed at anything—just to see if you get lucky?

Everyone has a champion trader inside. It's just a matter of knowledge, desire, and commitment. Most of all, you must believe in your own abilities. I assure you that you can accomplish much more than you think you can in trading, and with far less risk than the so-called experts would have you believe. But until you accept that winning is a choice, you will not be able to realize your full potential. Nor will you be in control of your destiny, because you have not taken full responsibility for the outcome; therefore, you are not fully empowered. **Those who choose to win seek successful role models, develop a road map for success, and accept setbacks as valuable teachers. They put a plan into action, learn from their results, and make adjustments until they achieve victory.**

Winners are people who can't stand not to win. Some start off that way, while others eventually get fed up with being mediocre and decide that they're not going to accept falling short of their dreams anymore. This attitude probably goes against what you heard as a child: *Don't be a sore loser.* In my experience, you show me a "good" loser and I'll show you someone who is likely to lose. If you want to trade like a champion, you need to think like one. Until you convince yourself that success is a choice, you're a defeated winner. It doesn't mean that you are a loser as a person; it simply means that you have not yet learned or accepted the truth about winning. **Champions don't leave greatness to chance. They decide that they are going to be winners, and they live each day with that goal in focus.**

In 1990, I made the choice to become a champion stock investor. That was nearly seven years *after* I made my first trade. That's right, seven years! I dabbled for almost a decade. And as you might guess, up to that point, my results were what you would expect from someone who dabbles. Then in March of 1990, I decided to make a firm commitment to become the best stock trader in the world. I've been working at it ever since, and the rest is history.

A TALE OF TWO WOLVES

There are two types of traders inside you and me and everyone. One I call the builder—disciplined and process-driven. The builder is focused on procedure and perfecting the method. The builder trusts that the results will come if he gets the process right. Mistakes are viewed as teachers, constantly providing valuable lessons in a continuous feedback loop. When the builder makes a mistake, it's taken as encouragement: *That's one I won't make again.* Ever optimistic, the builder looks forward to the day when results are achieved—good or bad—because the process is constantly being improved.

The other trader is what I call the wrecking ball. Ego-driven, the wrecking ball is fixated on results; if they don't come right away, he gets discouraged. If a mistake is made, the wrecking ball beats up on himself or looks for someone or something else to blame. If a strategy doesn't produce winning results quickly or it goes through a difficult period, the wrecking ball tosses it aside and looks for a new strategy, never really committing to the process. A wrecking ball, as you might guess, has tons of excuses and rarely takes ownership of the outcome—and as a result, never builds anything lasting or wonderful.

But remember what I said in the beginning. You are not one or the other. You have *both* the builder and the wrecking ball inside you, just as every human being has the capacity for love and compassion, and also for hatred and harm. So, which one is going to determine your results: the builder or the wrecking ball?

To answer that, I refer to one of my favorite stories told by Pema Chödrön in her book *Taking the Leap: Freeing Ourselves from Old Habits and Fears*: "A Native American grandfather was speaking to his grandson about violence and cruelty in the world and how it comes about. He said it was as if two wolves were fighting in his heart. One wolf was vengeful and angry, and the other wolf was understanding and kind. The young man asked his grandfather which wolf would win the fight in his heart. And the grandfather answered, 'The one that wins will be the one I choose to feed.'"

So it will be with you. I consider myself to be an enlightened trader. First, I recognize that I have both the builder and the wrecking ball within me. But, I choose to feed the builder and starve the wrecking ball. To be mindful of this daily is even more important than a strategy or the mechanics of trading. Because even a good strategy will do you no good if you feed the wrecking ball.

One of my favorite movie scenes is from *Two for the Money*, when Walter Abrams (played by Al Pacino), a degenerate gambler who runs a New York tout service (for betting on sports), attends a Gamblers Anonymous meeting with his new hotshot handicapper Brandon Lang (who goes by the name John Anthony) (played by Matthew McConaughey). After listening to Leon, one of the ex-gambler-attendees, speak, Walter gives the following speech—very funny and entertaining, and also very true:

> I know where you're coming from, Leon—believe me, I know. I heard your story, and it's something I can relate to. If I learned anything, it's that gambling is not your problem, not even close. I don't know how to say this without sounding a little rude, but, you're a lemon, Leon! Like a bad car, there's something inherently defective in you—and you, and me, and all of us in this room; we're all lemons. We look like everybody else, but what makes us different is our defect.
>
> You see, most gamblers when they go to gamble they go to win. When we go to gamble, we go to lose. Subconsciously, me . . . I never feel better or more alive than when they're raking the chips away! Not bringing them in. And everybody in here knows what I'm talking about. Even when we win, it's just a matter of time before we give it all back.

> But when we lose—now there's another story. When we
> lose, and I'm talking about the kind of loss that makes your ass—
> pucker up to the size of a decimal point. You know what I mean?
> You just re-created the worse possible nightmare this side
> of malignant cancer, for the twentieth time! And you suddenly
> realize . . . hey, I'm still here. I'm still breathing. I'm still alive.
> Us lemons, we f— shit up all the time on purpose . . . because
> we consistently need to remind ourselves we're alive. Leon, gam-
> bling is not your problem. It's this f— up need to feel something,
> to convince yourself that you exist! That's the problem.

In this book, you will learn the important tools necessary to put yourself on the road to successful trading. But before success can show up in the physical world, it must be achieved in the mind first. I know—from experience. Growing up poor with little education, I had virtually no resources. As a result, I had to learn how to rise above a poverty mentality—a mindset that was working against me. But you don't have to be poor to have a poverty mentality. Many people are trapped in fears of scarcity, or they feel undeserving because of their past or because of some falsehood they hold as true. You can even be rich, but if you don't enjoy life's journey and you lack passion, your life will be marginal. That unhappiness is the result of a poverty mentality.

If you put your heart, soul, and mind into something, then why not do everything you can to succeed in a big way? If you work hard and approach trading intelligently, you deserve success. But it takes persistence and the right mental attitude. If you're not open to having complete control over your financial destiny, then you probably shouldn't even read this book. Why? Because this book is all about taking ownership of your trading and your life and accepting full responsibility for your results. Without taking 100 percent responsibility, how can you cultivate a 100 percent ability to respond effectively?

The success blueprint in these pages has worked for me and for many others who have followed in my footsteps. It can and will work for you, but only if you're open to new ideas and accept the reality that becoming a champion stock trader is not about being gifted or having a degree in finance from an Ivy League school. It starts with the empowering belief that winning is without a doubt a choice. If you can believe that, then you just learned lesson number one: *Don't be a Leon.*

ALIGN YOUR INNER COMPASS

Would you mug a little old lady to become a super-successful stock trader? I bet that question caught you completely off guard! The real question is: why wouldn't you do that? The answer: because it goes against your belief system—your values and standards.

The key to winning at anything is having a belief in your own abilities, and aligning your belief system with your actions. I can assure you that you will never reach your full potential until you learn to act in sync with what you believe. Do you hold the belief that in order to make big returns, you must take big risks? If you do, then a low-risk, high-reward strategy may not resonate with you. With trading, if your beliefs are out of sync with your strategy, an inner conflict will hold you back and make success nearly impossible.

For example, if I were to attempt to use a system that held onto large losses that were offset by larger, infrequent gains, I would most certainly fail, even if that system was profitable and worked for someone else. I simply wouldn't be able to follow it for very long; I wouldn't have the confidence to stick through the losses because it goes against my belief about risk.

If my strategy makes sense to you, great! Adopt it. It will certainly point you in the right direction and start you off with sound rules. Then it's up to you to take action and use good judgment. Whatever strategy you choose, make sure you believe in what you are doing so you can fully commit to it and avoid self-sabotage.

Did you ever do something and then say to yourself, "What the heck is wrong with me? Why did I just do that when I know I shouldn't?" That's a red flag that you need to get in sync with your belief system because, in the long run, the belief system always wins. To be super successful, your actions must be aligned with your beliefs. Congruency is the goal.

MODEL SUCCESS

As you may already know from my first book, my Specific Entry Point Analysis (SEPA®) strategy is predicated on a Leadership Profile® for identifying promising stock candidates. Using historical data from as far back as the late 1800s, SEPA® develops a blueprint of the characteristics shared by superperformance stocks. It is based on an ongoing effort to identify the qualities and attributes of the most successful stocks of the past to determine what makes a stock likely to dramatically outperform its peers in the future. What I've done with SEPA® is simply model success.

Many years ago, when I was in my twenties, I went to a course given by Anthony Robbins (one of the most well-known motivators and an expert in human behavior) and learned a very valuable lesson. **If you want to paint like Leonardo da Vinci, first you need to learn to think like him. Because where the mind goes, everything else will eventually follow.** If I wanted to follow in the footsteps of the all-time great traders, I had to learn all I could about them, until I could think like they did. And so, I began to read books and study legendary traders. I wanted to get into their heads, to think like they did, so that I could model their success. I read these books over and over so I could fully internalize the information.

I'm not suggesting that success in trading means becoming a carbon copy of someone else. But before you can master a concept, you must truly own the knowledge. Why try to reinvent the wheel when there is a valuable body of knowledge to build upon? In 1677, Sir Isaac Newton famously said, "If I have seen further, it is by standing on the shoulders of giants." Think of Picasso, one of the pioneers of Cubism. He studied classic techniques at art academies, including under his father's tutelage. But once he truly owned the rules, he could go beyond them.

Many years ago, one of my first trainees was a young man from Canada named Darren. (Some of you may have met him at one of our Master Trader Workshops.) Darren was more than a protégé; he was like the son I never had—even though he is only a bit younger than me. Darren wanted to learn my approach to trading, and he was committed to modeling my belief system to achieve the type of results I was producing.

For a while, Darren stayed at my house. While he was there, he began to study and adopt my habits, subtly at first and then more noticeably. I was bodybuilding at the time, so I ate a very specific diet. Darren was a relatively skinny guy and didn't lift weights, but he started eating the exact same meals I did and taking my vitamins and protein powders. At first I didn't think much of it, but then I noticed he began to adopt what were some pretty personal habits.

As a bodybuilder, I would routinely clip and shave the hair off my body. One day, while I was in the living room, I heard a buzzing sound. I followed it to the bathroom door. I knocked on the door and asked Darren what he was doing. When he opened the door, he was standing there with his pale, skinny legs completely hairless.

"What are you doing?" I asked him. "You're not a bodybuilder!"

"I don't care," he told me. "If you shave, I'm shaving. Whatever you do, I do. If you sit in the green chair, I sit in a green chair. If I want to trade like you, I have to think like you. To do that, I'm going to do everything you do!"

My first thought was "This kid is insane." Then I realized he was a genius! He intuitively grasped a concept that I had just come to understand about the importance of modeling someone's belief system. Darren knew that if you truly want to understand someone, you must become like that person—walk in the person's shoes, as the saying goes. Darren's commitment to learn all he could from me led him to not only study my strategies, but also adopt my disciplines. Soon he was going to the gym on a regular basis and even started lifting weights.

Over time, Darren's discipline paid off. He was up 160 percent his very first year trading with me; he then had multiple years of triple-digit gains on his own and went on to become a highly successful stock trader. He had his unwavering focus to thank for that success. He was willing to be all-in, with a single-mindedness I've never seen in anyone else. For him, perception was everything.

EMBRACE THE PROCESS

As I sat down to write this Introduction, I received an e-mail from a trader who had read my first book. While he was very complimentary about the material, he admitted to having difficulty trading. "I just can't put it together," he wrote.

Then he began to blame himself, figuring that he's just not cut out to be a trader. Reading between the lines, I could tell this guy had clearly convinced himself that winning big is something that other people achieve, but not him.

I took it personally—and in the best possible way.

I want this individual and everyone like him to jettison the notion that, somehow, they aren't cut out for trading. If you ever get to a point where you are questioning your ability, you must shed the belief that there is something missing inside of you—some intelligence, aptitude, or special talent—that keeps you from "getting it." This trader (like you, like me) has everything he needs to become successful, provided he is willing to do one thing. You guessed it: accept that winning is a choice; the powerful belief that everything builds from. Until you do, I can assure you that success will be a hit and miss affair, and superperformance in stocks will elude you.

No one starts out at the top; there is no special God-given talent for trading as if the human genome had a strand of DNA just for speculators. No one is a "natural" stock investor. In fact, I'd say that, trading is one of the most *unnatural* things one can do. I'm not alone in this thinking. In response to people who thought "somehow that others are just born to invest," superstar investor Peter Lynch said in his book *One Up on Wall Street*, "There was no ticker tape above my cradle, nor did I teethe on the stock pages."

You may have heard about a team of psychologists in Berlin, Germany, who in the early 1990s studied violin students. Specifically, they studied their practice habits in childhood, adolescence, and adulthood. All the violinists had begun playing at roughly five years of age with similar practice times. However, at age eight, practice times began to diverge. By age twenty, the elite performers averaged more than 10,000 hours of practice each, while the less able performers had only 4,000 hours of practice.

Interestingly, no "naturally gifted" performers emerged. If natural talent had played a role, we would expect some of the "naturals" to float to the top of the elite level with fewer practice hours than everyone else. But the data showed otherwise. The psychologists found a direct statistical relationship between hours of practice and achievement. No shortcuts. No naturals. The elite had more than double the practice hours of the less capable performers.

The bottom line is you're going to have to work to get great at trading, and it's going to take some time, but the payoff is well worth the personal investment. Whatever gifts or ability someone might have been born with, success in the market comes from a concerted effort and a willingness to allow the learning curve to unfold, no matter how long it takes.

It's not just putting in the hours that will make you successful; it's the persistent intention to improve by examining your results, tweaking your approach, and making incremental progress. In his book *The Talent Code*, Daniel Coyle refers to this process as "deep practice"—not just doing the same thing over and over, but using feedback to make adjustments and making practice more meaningful.

Just because you make the decision to be great at stock trading doesn't mean you will produce great results immediately. Would you walk into a courtroom after a few months of law school and try a case with little or no experience? If you did, would you be surprised if you lost the case? Or, would you attempt to perform an operation having attended only two premed classes? If you did, heaven forbid, would you be surprised if the patient wasn't cured? These scenarios, of course, seem utterly ridiculous. But even if I were to walk into the kitchen at a McDonald's restaurant and try to work the fryer, I would not even know how to turn it on. Why? It's not because I lack intelligence or a special talent, but simply because I have not yet acquired the necessary knowledge and experience.

Yet some people open a brokerage account and expect to immediately reap stellar returns. When they don't, they make excuses, give up, or start taking huge risks. Rarely does it occur to them that they need specialized knowledge and the patience to acquire it.

I was a terrible trader when I first started out. The success I eventually achieved didn't come from natural talent. Unconditional persistence and learned discipline brought me where I am today. And I know, even today, if I break my discipline, I could easily go from success to failure.

Those who succeed big at anything all have the same attitude: You keep going until it happens or you die trying. Quitting is not an option. If you don't go in with that attitude, then you will likely give up when the going gets tough.

DEFINE YOURSELF

Your strategy is the one that works for you, not every time, but over time. It takes the same commitment you would make in a relationship. How good a marriage do you think you would have if you cheated on your spouse? A trading strategy is the same; you need to be faithful to it for it to give back to you.

Odds are that you won't be good at value investing, growth investing, swing trading, and day trading. If you try to do them all, you will most likely end up a mediocre jack-of-all-trades. To reap the benefits of one strategy, you have to sacrifice the others. You will enjoy market cycles when your trading style outperforms other styles. But you won't overcome less favorable phases by adopting a different style each time you run into difficulty. To become great at anything, you must be focused and specialize; you must avoid what's known as "style drift."

Style drift comes from not clearly defining your strategy and goals. As a result, you won't stay with your approach through thick and thin. If you are a short-term trader, you must recognize that selling a stock for a quick profit only to watch it go on to double in price is of no real concern to you. You operate in a particular zone of a stock's price continuum, and someone else may operate in a totally different area of the curve. Both can be successful! However, if you're a longer-term investor, there will be many times when you make a decent short-term gain only to give it all back in the pursuit of a larger move. The key is to focus on a particular style. Once you define your style and objectives, it becomes much easier to stick to a plan and attain success. In time, you will be rewarded for your sacrifice with your own specialty.

Prioritize the Prize

In trading—as in anything in life—it's not just about knowing what you want, it's about knowing what you want *first*. The secret to success is prioritizing your desires. People generally want the same things: love, happiness, freedom, friendship, respect, financial rewards, and so on. It's safe to say that everybody wants the good things in life. I'm referring here to your specific goals: whether it's becoming a successful trader, a gourmet chef, or a champion tennis player. You could become all three.

But the trick to having everything in life is to go after your goals, one at a time. Figure out what you want *first*, and don't move on to the next thing until you accomplish your first goal. Why? If you spread yourself too thin, you won't succeed big at anything and will never experience anything fully. Specialists get paid well, while those who know a little about many things make good conversation at parties.

Mastery requires sacrifices; therefore, something must come first. Make a list, prioritize, and pursue accordingly: Focus, achieve, and then move to the next big goal.

The advice I'm giving you here is to be unbalanced. Yes, you read that correctly. To be highly successful at something, you must be unbalanced. This runs contrary to the notion these days that you must have balance in your life, especially where work and family life are concerned. That's certainly the goal, and in my life today, I don't put anyone or anything before my wife and daughter. But if you are pursuing superperformance in stocks, a partial effort will likely produce only partial results.

When I was new to trading, I was unbalanced, and purposefully so. I was like an Olympian who trains 12 hours a day. I ate, drank, and breathed trading. It was all I thought about. It was total immersion in a one-dimensional life. If that sounds scary, maybe being a top super-performing trader is not what you truly desire. But that doesn't mean you can't improve your trading and enjoy the benefits of investing, even as a part-time investor.

There are plenty of other examples of professionals who, during an intense period of training, are similarly unbalanced. Think of the medical resident who puts in 16-hour days and catches only a few hours of sleep on a cot in the ER.

You cannot achieve mastery with a mediocre effort. You need to give it your all, and then some. It will not always be this way. But in the beginning, as you devote yourself to something as challenging as trading, you must put in the work and stay laser focused. If you want big returns in the stock market, you must make your trading a priority.

TAKE ACTION

Delay is the worst thing you can do when trying to accomplish a goal. People convince themselves that they'll do something when everything is "perfect." While I certainly do encourage you to learn all you can, I don't consider that a delay. When you walk around thinking, *I'll start—someday, maybe soon, just not right now*, that's delay.

I received an e-mail from someone who read my first book and said he was "getting ready" to follow my rules. But first, he was trying to day-trade; he felt that he needed to make more mistakes before he got really disciplined. After that, he would be ready to commit to my approach. I have no idea what that means, except that he had not yet decided to practice correctly.

The longer you put off committing to something, the easier it is to delay it even more, because the closer you get to a challenge, delay shouts all the louder. The counterpunch to delay is action. You must take action or nothing will materialize. If you wait for the perfect time or when you think you have all the answers, you may never get started. It's better to do something imperfectly than to do nothing flawlessly. You can dream, you can think positively, you can plan and set goals, but unless you act, nothing will materialize. It's not enough to have knowledge, a dream, or passion; it's what you do with what you know that counts. The best time to get started is now!

Go Beyond Your Comfort Zone

In life, there seems to be a universal truth I call the CLUM principle; comfortable equals less and uncomfortable equals more. Potential and possibility reside in the fertile field of the unknown. Moving outside your comfort zone doesn't mean taking on big risks. It means you will have to stretch yourself and do things that, at first, may feel unnatural or counterintuitive. Fortunately, you don't have to jump from the safe and familiar directly to what feels completely impossible, as if you dove off the cliffs at Acapulco while you were still learning to swim. It's a process of gaining proficiency—and comfort—along the way, expanding your comfort zone.

Picture a series of concentric circles; at the center is your current comfort zone. You start in the center, at "ring 1," which is what you already know. From that initial phase, you gain some experience, learn about yourself, and begin to hone your discipline. But ring 1 is only a starting point. You can't stay there permanently if you want to achieve phenomenal success in trading or anything worthwhile.

Think of the tremendous effort involved in learning to play a musical instrument or to become good at sports. It takes hours of practice and feedback from good coaches and teachers who will help you improve your technique. With time and commitment, your skill level advances to the point that you're able to play Beethoven or swing for the fences with the heavier hitters. **As a stock trader, when you strip off what feels natural and learn to do what feels unnatural, you become supernatural.** You can't jump from ring 1 to ring 4, though; you need to put in the necessary time and effort to gain competence and confidence. If you rush without building a foundation of skills and experiences, you'll invite disaster.

Whatever the endeavor, as you move from beginner to more advanced, you stretch yourself from ring 1 to ring 2. Now, ring 2 is your new or expanded comfort zone. As a trader at ring 2, perhaps you've further refined your selection criteria and can now take bigger positions without being exposed to undue risk. With more experience and information, you move into ring 3, and ring 4 becomes your next target. And so it goes.

As Ralph Waldo Emerson said, "The mind, once stretched by a new idea, never returns to its original dimensions." In the same way, as you successfully expand beyond your previous limitations, you won't have the desire or need to go back to the small place of your original thinking. Looking back, you will be pleasantly surprised by how much you've grown and matured in your trading. What had seemed so difficult, even impossible, is now well within your reach and part of your new, expanded comfort zone. With practice and discipline, this new, expanded level of competency becomes axiomatic to the point of being second nature. This is how mastery is built, one step at a time.

PURSUE THE THIRD STAGE OF KNOWLEDGE

There are three basic levels of knowledge. The first level is when an *idea* is presented to you by someone else. Someone tells you something, and you evaluate it against your own opinions. You might have mixed feelings about this information; maybe you agree, disagree, or don't really know what to make of it. The second level is when you become convinced that what you have been told is true. Now, it's a *belief.* A belief is stronger than an idea, but it is still not the strongest level of knowledge. The third level is a knowing—the most powerful form of awareness. This is the knowledge that you carry within yourself. It is what you know to be true because you've experienced it firsthand.

In this book, you will receive many ideas. Maybe you will move them to the second level when you become convinced that what I'm telling you is true. I have spent many years of trial and error, sweat and tears. As you accept and embody these ideas and incorporate them into your trading, they will, indeed, become part of your body of knowledge—instinctive, automatic, and unquestionable. Your goal is to achieve the third level of knowledge, a knowing that can only be acquired through practice and personal experience.

There are no shortcuts. No matter how many books you read or how many workshops you attend, you can't force experience. Don't get discouraged if you're not getting big results right away. No matter how much knowledge you soak up or how smart you are, you still need to put in your time at the University of Wall Street.

When I first started, it took me six long years to become profitable. Through those challenging years, though, I stuck with my strategy. I didn't jump from one approach to another as if there were some magic formula out there and the secret was finding it. As stated earlier, I decided on a strategy that made sense to me and then concentrated on improving my ability to execute it. I stayed the course, remained steadfastly disciplined, and stuck to the rules. Persistence is more important than knowledge, and victory comes to those who persist, as long as you are learning from your experiences.

Acquiring the correct knowledge through involvement does not have to be difficult or stressful. With sound rules and a strategy, you willingly allow the process to unfold—by first embracing the process and then learning from it. You trust that things are happening normally, and everything is unfolding as it should.

Now We Can Begin

You've gotten this far, to the end of the Introduction—one toe in the water. Are you going to take the plunge?

This brings us back to where we started this discussion. You have a choice—a decision to make—whether you are going to win or lose. First, you must declare that you are deserving of success. As I pointed out earlier, there are people who undermine themselves because they do not believe that they deserve success. Maybe it was something they did when they were younger that they now regret. Or maybe it's the way they grew up. Whatever the reason, they are holding onto a faulty belief system that tells them they are not worthy of success. If that resonates with you, then it's time to forgive yourself, put the past behind you, and move forward.

You deserve to have success and passion in your life—a big goal worth committing yourself to. You deserve to create and do something that sparks your interest and challenges you intellectually. Trading is certainly one of those challenges. It goes far beyond any financial rewards; it is a lifetime of self-mastery, overcoming ego and fears. On the other hand, there are people who believe they are entitled to success, whether because of their family name, background, education, or whatever "pedigree" they wear on their sleeve. The market will teach them otherwise, and it will probably be a tough lesson. Success comes one way: hard work and humility. In the stock market, those who are not humble are destined to be humbled.

Change, though, happens in an instant. Just like a smoker can become an ex-smoker by putting out the last cigarette or an alcoholic can put down a drink and never touch a drop again, so it is with limiting beliefs or behaviors. You can flip the switch on your dreams and your destiny by taking charge and taking responsibility, starting today.

But first, you have to decide to decide.

Superperformance trader or not, it's your choice. Decide right here and right now. There is no better time. Maybe that's why you picked up this book. Maybe that's why everything that has come before in your life and all you want to achieve in the future have converged into this moment. If you don't love your life, it is because someone else influenced it more than you did. Decide now! Then turn the page.

ALWAYS GO IN WITH A PLAN

Virtually every endeavor—playing a sport, building a house, jack-hammering a street, running for political office, or performing a surgical operation—requires a plan before you get started. A contractor wouldn't even start to dig the foundation for a building without having blueprints. Before every game, the coach of your favorite sports team drafts a game plan and presents it to the players. A surgeon has test results, MRI imaging, and a surgical plan before making the first incision.

If you want success in the stock market, before you do anything, you should develop a plan. The *how* of your plan resides in a series of concrete guides for action. Most investors, though, have no real plan. Or, worse yet, they have a poor plan based on faulty notions and unrealistic ideas about investing. They get a tip from a broker or they hear something on TV, or maybe someone who supposedly knows somebody tells them that a stock is going to take off. And just like that, thousands of dollars are on the line, without a tangible plan.

How smart is that?

Trading is serious business with real money on the line. Why would you go into it without a well-thought-out plan of action? Yet, most people do. The ease of entry into the stock market—no license or training required; just open a brokerage account and go—may give people the false impression that trading is easy. Or, perhaps they think their odds of succeeding without much thought are far better than they really are. Whatever the reason, I've seen people invest $100,000 in a stock with less research than when they buy an $800 flat screen TV. They'll commit thousands of dollars to a stock because of a tip from a friend of a friend, without spending much time if any on research and planning. Greed takes over, and all they can see is the upside, without much thought about the downside or if the unthinkable happens!

HAVE A PROCESS

When I first started trading, I had no real plan at all. My only "strategy," if I can call it that, was to follow that old axiom: "Buy low and sell high." I thought that meant to buy stocks that were down, figuring that what goes down must go back up. I'd buy big-name companies when they were depressed, because I'd been told, "You can't go wrong with AT&T or General Electric." Buying these stocks when they dropped seemed like a great idea to me back then, because I believed they were less risky and eventually had to go up. Wrong!

In time, I learned that there is no such thing as a safe stock. That's like saying there's such a thing as a safe race car. Like race cars, all stocks are risky. Just because a company is a household name or a well-established business with experienced management doesn't mean it's a great stock to buy. During severe bear markets, even "high-quality" companies can get slaughtered; some even go bankrupt. General Electric topped in 2000 and fell from $60 per share to under $6. That's more than a 90 percent decline in value! By 2016, the stock had only recovered half the drop. Sixteen years later, investors that bought the blue-chip conglomerate were still sitting with a 50 percent loss. And that happened investing in what is considered to be one of the highest quality companies in the entire world.

The list of casualties among big "safe" investment-grade companies is endless. Many of the poor-performing stocks I bought during those early days got pulverized before I threw in the towel with losses that took large chunks out of my trading capital and my confidence. Does this sound familiar?

It didn't take me very long to realize I had to come up with a plan for buying stocks, but more important, I needed a plan for dealing with the inherent risk that all stocks carry. A plan lays the ground rules of your trade. It is the what, why, when, and how of trading. Having a plan won't guarantee success on every trade, but it will help you manage risk, minimize losses, nail down profits when you have them, and handle unexpected events with decisive action, which over time will dramatically improve your chances of success. **By defining my parameters ahead of time, I establish a basis for knowing whether my plan is working or not.**

Have a process, any process, but have a process. Then you have the basis from which to work, make adjustments, and perfect your process.

Key Elements of a Trading Plan

- An entry "mechanism" that determines precisely what triggers a buy decision
- How you are going to deal with risk; what will you do if the trade moves against you, or if the reason you bought the stock changes suddenly?
- How you're going to lock in your profits
- How will you position size, and when will you decide to reallocate funds?

HOPE IS NOT A PLAN

A trading plan gives you a baseline of expectation. That way, you know if your trade is working out, or if something has gone wrong. Wishing and hoping are not the same as planning. As fellow Market Wizard Ed Seykota put it, "Be sensitive to the subtle differences between 'intuition' and 'into wishing.'" Hope is not a strategy. **Without a plan, you can only rationalize. Often you will tell yourself to be patient when you should be selling, or you may panic during a natural pullback and then miss out on a huge stock move.**

Defining what you expect to happen ahead of time allows you to judge if your trades are working and delivering "on time." To use one of my favorite analogies, it's the difference between having a schedule and wondering when the next train will pull into the station. If you take the 6:05 scheduled train every morning, but one day it's not there by 6:15, you won't think much of the minor delay. If the train is not there by 7:30, you know something is really wrong and you should probably come up with an alternative mode of transportation.

In the same way, expectations for your stock trade are the "schedule." If the profit you're expecting doesn't materialize, you shouldn't just sit there waiting with dead money for months and months while the stock goes nowhere and better opportunities present themselves. You'll know what to do because your plan tells you. With a well-thought-out plan, you will be able to determine if the proverbial train is on schedule, or if there's a disruption in your timeline that is reason for concern.

CONTINGENCY PLANNING

The best way to ensure stock market success is to have contingency plans—using a "what if" process—and update them as you encounter new scenarios and build your contingency playbook. In the wake of the 9/11 terrorist attacks on the World Trade Center, many financial firms decentralized their core IT systems. Merrill Lynch moved its primary data center to Staten Island, where it runs on a separate electrical grid to mitigate the potential loss of power in one area. The New York site now functions as a backup.

Your goal as a stock speculator is preparedness, to trade with few surprises. To do so, you need to develop a dependable way to handle virtually every situation that may occur. Having events and circumstances thought out in advance is a key to managing risk effectively and building your capital account.

The mark of a professional is proper preparation. **Before I make a trade, I have already worked out responses to meet virtually any conceivable development that may take place.** And, if and when a new set of circumstances present themselves, I add them to my contingency plans. As new unexpected issues present themselves, the contingency plan playbook is expanded. By implementing contingency planning, you can take swift, decisive action the instant one of your positions changes its behavior or is hit with an unexpected event.

Disappointments can trigger your contingency plans, especially where to exit the trade at a loss and when to protect your profit. And while you're at it, have a disaster plan. Mine covers all the things I'd never want to happen while I'm in a trade, such as losing power or my Internet connection. I once experienced an entire brokerage firm go down system wide. As a result, I maintain a second account so I could go short against my longs should the same scenario occur. Having a disaster plan gives me peace of mind, because should the unthinkable happen, I know exactly how to respond immediately.

You should have contingency plans for the following:

1.   Where you will get out if the position goes against you
2.   What the stock must do to be considered for purchase again in the event you get stopped out of the trade
3.   Criteria for selling into strength and nailing down a decent gain
4.   When to sell into weakness to protect your profit
5.   How you will handle catastrophic situations and sudden changes that require swift decisive action under pressure

Your contingency plan should include the following elements:

•   Initial stop-loss. Before buying a stock, I establish in advance a maximum stop-loss—the price at which I will exit the position if it moves against me. The moment the price hits the stop-loss, I sell the position without question. Once I'm out of the stock, I can then evaluate the situation with a clear head. The initial stop-loss is most relevant in the early stages of a trade. Once a stock advances, the sell point should be raised to protect your profit with the use of a trailing stop or back stop.
•   Reentry criteria. Some stocks will set up constructively and attract buyers, but then they quickly undergo a correction or sharp pull-

back that stops you out. This tends to occur when the market is suffering general weakness or high volatility. Often, a stock with strong fundamentals can reset after such a pullback, forming a new base and a proper buy point. Very often, the second setup is even stronger than the first because the stock has fought its way back and, along the way, shaken out another batch of weak holders.

You shouldn't assume that a stock will reset if it stops you out; you should always protect yourself and cut your loss. But if you get stopped out of your position, don't automatically discard it as a future buy candidate. If the stock still has all the characteristics of a potential winner, look for a reentry point. The first time around your timing may have been a bit off. It could take two or even three tries to catch a big winner. This is a trait of a professional trader. Amateurs get scared of positions that stop them out once or twice, professionals are objective and dispassionate. They assess each trade on its merits of risk versus reward; they look at each trade setup as a new opportunity.

- Selling at a profit. Once a stock purchase you made shows you a decent profit, generally a multiple of your stop-loss, you should not allow that position to turn into loss. For instance, let's say your stop-loss is set at 7 percent. If you have a 20 percent gain in a stock, you should never let that position give up all that profit and produce a loss. To guard against that, you could move up your stop-loss to breakeven or trail a stop to lock in the majority of the gain. You may feel foolish breaking even or taking a small profit on a position that was previously a bigger gain; however, you will feel even worse if you let a nice profit turn into a loss.

There are two ways to sell at a profit. Once you buy a stock, there are two basic scenarios for selling and nailing down your profit. The ideal is selling into strength, after the stock has done what you hoped it would do. The other is selling into weakness, because the stock reversed down to a level that you want to protect. (Where, when, and how to sell will be discussed at length in Section 9.)

Selling into strength is a learned practice of professional traders. It's important to recognize when a stock is running up too rapidly and may be exhausting itself. You can unload your position easily when buyers are plentiful. Or you could sell into the first signs of weakness immediately after such a price run has started to break down. You need to have a plan for both selling into strength and selling into weakness.

- Disaster plan. This could turn out to be the most important part of your contingency planning. It deals with such issues as what to do if your Internet connection goes down or your power fails. Do you have a backup system? Or what will your response be if you wake up tomorrow morning and learn that the stock you bought yesterday is set to gap down huge because the company is being investigated by the Securities and Exchange Commission and the CEO has skipped the country with embezzled funds. What do you do?

Priorities in Order of Importance

a. Limit your loss. Define how much you're willing to risk and set a stop-loss.

b. Protect your line. Once the stock price moves up and you have a decent profit (generally after the first natural reaction and a recovery to new highs), you should then move up the stop near your breakeven point.

c. Protect your profit. Don't allow good-size gains to slip away; use a trailing stop or a back stop.

Before I enter a new stock position (Figure 1-1), the first thing I do is decide (Point a) where I'm going to cut my loss if the trade moves against me. Then, as the stock moves up, my priority changes to protecting my breakeven price (Point b). If I'm fortunate to have a decent gain, my priority shifts again, this time to protecting my profit (Point c).

The important role contingency planning plays is that it enables you to make good decisions when you're under fire—when you need it the most. Contingency planning allows you to have a psychological strategy that is as robust as your trading strategy, as well as a trading strategy that has built-in responses to potential situations that could, if not prepared for, lead to competing thoughts at the precise time you need to implement instant, unbiased action.

Contingency planning is an ongoing process. As you experience new problems, a procedure should be created to deal with them, which then becomes part of your contingency plans. You're never going to have all the answers, but you can cover most of the bases to the point where your reward outweighs your risk, and that's the key.

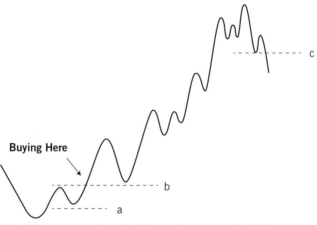

Figure 1-1 Know your trade priorities and how you will limit losses and protect profits as they accumulate.

WHAT DOES A PLAN LOOK LIKE IN REAL LIFE?

Planning is not limited to just certain strategies. Regardless if you're a value trader, a momentum trader, a long-term investor, or a day trader, you need to have a plan of attack and a plan of defense. Don't get into the market without a plan!

Here are some of the assumptions and expectations that go into my trading plan. When I buy a stock, I expect it to move up pretty quickly after I buy it. The reason is that my setup, which, as we'll discuss later in the book, utilizes something I call the volatility contraction pattern, or VCP, which is where volatility and volume contract, resulting in the development of the line of least resistance. Following my strategy, if a stock breaks out of the VCP to the upside, that's a positive sign. After that breakout, I'm looking for a few things that will let me know if the trade is working out according to my plan.

LOOK FOR FOLLOW-THROUGH BUYING

The key to trading breakouts is to determine the probability of a sustained advance versus just a short-term rally that fizzles away. The first thing I would like to see after a breakout from a base is multiple days of follow-through action, the more the better. **The best trades emerge and rally for several days on increased volume. This is how you differentiate institutional buying from retail buying.** If big institutions are in there accumulating a position, it will likely happen over a number of days with persistent buying. On the other hand, smaller retail buying may break a stock out, but the buying will not be enough to hold the stock up for very long. The best indication that you're going to make big money on a trade is when you're at a profit right away, and the stock follows through for several days on good volume (Figure 1-2).

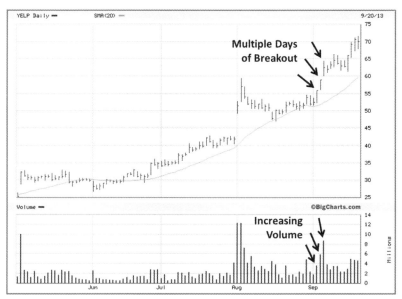

Figure 1-2   Yelp (YELP) 2013. Stock emerged from a five-week base with multiple days of follow-through on increased volume—a sign of institutional accumulation.

HOLD TENNIS BALLS AND SELL EGGS

It's important that you learn how to distinguish the difference between normal price behavior and abnormal. This will help you determine when to hold and when to fold. In the 1980s, I had a chance to hear William M. B. Berger (founder of Berger Funds) speak about stock investing. Bill said eight very important words: "I want to own tennis balls, not eggs." Those words turned out to be worth millions to me.

Once a stock moves though a proper pivot point and triggers my buy price, I watch the stock very closely to see how it acts. **Determining whether the stock is a tennis ball or an egg will tell you whether you should continue holding it or not.** After a stock advances, the price at some point will experience a short-term pullback. If the stock is healthy, the pullbacks will be brief and soon met with buying support, which should push the stock to new highs within just days—bouncing back like a tennis ball.

Tennis ball action will generally occur after two to five days or even one to two weeks of pullback, followed by the stock bouncing back up again, taking out the most recent highs. This is valuable information when it occurs subsequent to the price emerging from a proper base.

Volume should contract during the pullback and then expand as the stock moves back into new highs. This is how you determine whether the stock is experiencing a *natural reaction* or abnormal activity that should raise concern. **Stocks under strong institutional accumulation almost always find support during the first few pullbacks over the course of several days to a couple of weeks after emerging from a sound structure.**

Often, a stock will emerge through a buy point and then pull back to or slightly below the initial breakout level; this will happen 40 to 50 percent of the time. This is normal as long as the stock recovers fairly quickly within a number of days or perhaps within one to two weeks. Minor reactions or pullbacks in price are natural and are bound to occur as the price advance runs its course. Sometimes the general market experiences a sharp decline just as the stock is emerging from a base, and the weakness pulls the stock back.

It's during these pullbacks that you get to see what the stock is really made of. Does it come bouncing back like a tennis ball (Figures 1-3 through 1-5), or does it go splat like an egg? The best stocks usually rebound the fastest. Once I buy a stock, if it meets my upside expectations very quickly and displays tennis ball action, I will probably hold it longer. This is not something I decide randomly; it's all part of my plan.

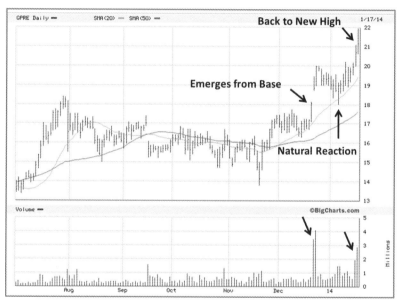

Figure 1-3   Green Plains (GPRE) 2013. +150% in eight months. The stock emerged from a base, pulled back for nine days (natural reaction), and then returned to new high ground on expanding volume (tennis ball action).

Figure 1-4   Netflix (NFLX) 2009. +525% in 21 months. The stock emerged from a six-month base with brief pullbacks of five and seven days respectively before turning back up into new high ground.

Figure 1-5   Lululemon Athletica (LULU) 2010. +245% in 18 months. After breaking out of a well-defined double bottom, the first two pullbacks were brief; the stock then moved convincingly into new high ground.

The Follow-Through Count

Another characteristic to look for as an indication that the trade is working out as planned is more up days than down days during the first week or two of a rally. I simply count the days up and the days down; the more up days the better. I want to see three up days out of four, or six up days out of eight—ideally seven or eight up days in a row. Stocks under institutional accumulation almost always display this type of price action, which is evidence that institutions are establishing big positions that can't be filled in only one day.

As a result, the stock should be "hard to buy," meaning you don't get much of an opportunity to get a better fill than the initial breakout price. Another nuance to look for during the initial rally phase is more days with good closes than bad closes (Figures 1-6 and 1-7). You want to see closes occurring in the upper half of the daily range more often than in the lower half. The only exception is during very tight price action when

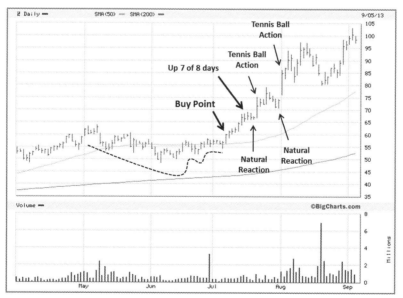

Figure 1-6   Zillow (Z) 2013. +182% in 12 months. The stock broke out of a base; up seven of eight days. Pullbacks were brief and met with support; the stock displayed excellent follow-through and tennis ball action.

Figure 1-7 Bitauto Holdings Ltd Ads (BITA) 2013. +478% in 11 months. Stock broke out of a base, up 4 out of 5 days; then pulled in for 2 days before moving back into new high ground, then trading up 8 out of 10 days.

volume contracts significantly and the range from high to low is minimal, which is also constructive.

Big winning stocks will display the following characteristics:

- Follow-through price action after a breakout
- More up days than down days and more up weeks than down weeks
- Tennis ball action—resilient price snapback after a pullback
- Strong volume on up days and up weeks compared to down days and down weeks
- More good closes than bad closes

WHEN NOT TO SELL AN "EXTENDED" STOCK

When my friend David Ryan was running the New USA Growth Fund with William O'Neil back in the mid-1990s, he noticed many stocks would break out of a base and quickly get "extended in price." His definition of "extended" is any stock that is up more than 10 percent from the most recent consolidation. David would never buy a stock that was extended, but he noticed some of these stocks would just keep going up, getting more and more extended. In many cases these stocks made tremendous gains.

Who continued to buy these stocks?

David figured it had to be big mutual funds or hedge funds that couldn't fill their positions in just one or two days. In some cases, it would take weeks for them to buy the amount they wanted. Their willingness to bid up the shares sparked David's curiosity and led him to study the signs of "big money" taking positions that could only be bought over multiple days. He compared these stocks to those that had smaller moves and quickly rolled over and went back down in price. After countless hours of studying and observation, and with the help of a terrific programmer named Rajneesh Gupta, he found some distinct characteristics.

David originally called the setup "ants." This is a term he made up to describe the annotations that would appear on the chart to indicate when the stock met the proper criteria; they were tiny marks right above the price bars. During a recent conversation, David told me an easy way to remember this setup is to refer to it as the "MVP indicator," which stands for momentum, volume, and price.

Stocks that continued much higher had the following characteristics that separated them from the rest (Figure 1-8):

- Momentum. The stock is up 12 out of 15 days.
- Volume. The volume increases 25 percent or more during the 15-day period.
- Price. The stock price is up 20 percent or more during the 15 days (the larger the move and the stronger the volume during these 15 days, the better).

David warns against buying a stock solely on these characteristics if the stock is extended. He says you should wait for a pullback (natural reaction) or a new base to form. However, sometimes a stock will have

Figure 1-8   Google (GOOGL) 2004. +625% in 40 months. The stock ran up from a buy point seven days in a row. Pullbacks were brief and met with support all the way from $52 to $100.

these MVP characteristics and not be extended. That can occur when the 15-day time frame begins near the bottom of a base. In that case, the stock is in position to be bought immediately. It's important to point out that this indicator is used in reverse as a sell signal when a stock is extended from a late stage base. I discuss this in Section 9, "When to Sell and Nail Down Profits."

Everyone wants an MVP like a Michael Jordan or a Peyton Manning on their team. David's MVP indicator can help you spot promising stocks, or maybe have you hold onto a position that is showing strong institutional interest dominated by "ants."

IF THINGS DON'T GO AS PLANNED

Every plan must account for negative developments. The reality is you will have many trades that do not work out as you expected. You must have a plan to deal with those situations and minimize the damage. **You**

should know the signs that a trade is problematic, which can tip you off it's time to exit the stock or reduce your position—in some cases even before it hits your stop. Maybe the stock's fundamentals deteriorate. Or maybe it's a good company, but your timing was off and a better technical setup will emerge later. But as for the trade you're in right now, if your expectations are not being met and the stock is not acting right, you need to recognize it. The following are a few "violations" that tell me a trade is not working according to my plan:

WATCH THE 20-DAY LINE
SOON AFTER A BASE BREAKOUT

Once a stock breaks out of a proper base and starts moving up, it should hold above its 20-day moving average; I don't want to see the price close below its 20-day line soon after a breakout. If that happens, it's a negative. I won't necessarily sell just for that reason alone. But my studies have shown that, after a stock breaks out of a proper VCP, if it closes below its 20-day moving average shortly thereafter, the probability of it being successful before stopping you out is cut in about half. If the stock closes below the 50-day line on heavy volume, it's an even worse sign. Remember, a close below the 20-day moving average is not significant on its own; it's when it occurs soon after a stock breaks out of a proper base that the 20-day line is noteworthy, particularly if additional violations are triggered.

THREE LOWER LOWS ON VOLUME
SHOULD GET YOUR ATTENTION

Another concern is when a stock puts in three lower lows that reverse a breakout—and, in particular, what happens on the third lower day and the following day. Three lower lows on increased volume is a red flag (Figure 1-9); however, if on the third lower day, buyers rush in and volume increases to the point that the stock actually closes higher or in the upper half of the range, I may stay in the trade. But if the stock closes with a third lower low and without supportive buying action, that's another strike against the trade, especially if the lower lows come on heavy volume.

Figure 1-9   WageWorks (WAGE) 2014. After a relatively low-volume breakout, the stock price failed to follow through and instead sold off, producing three lower lows on increasing volume and a close below the 20-day line.

Sometimes it takes four lower lows. The rule of thumb, however, is every consecutive lower low after the third becomes more and more ominous, and even much more so if volume is high. You should watch your stocks carefully when this occurs. A mild pullback on low volume can exceed three lower lows without reason for concern. However, when three or more lower lows occur and volume picks up, that's a violation. When this happens, you should watch your stock very closely. If the stock can't find support, beware!

When you combine these two scenarios soon after a breakout—a close below the 20-day moving average and a third lower low without supportive action, or worse, higher volume with a bad close—that trade has slim chances of success.

Low Volume *out*, High Volume *in* Is a Big Warning

Volume action could be a telltale sign of success or failure in a trade. Let's say you bought a stock as it broke out of a VCP pattern on what appeared to be pretty good volume. But if you bought that stock early in the trading day—say, after the first hour of trading—you can't be sure if it's going to be a high-volume day or not. What happens next will give you some indications of your likelihood of success.

At our 2014 Master Trader Workshop, three-time U.S. Investing Champion David Ryan said, "I want to be at a profit immediately. If I don't see a profit very soon after I buy the stock, I'm inclined to just get out." **If a stock breaks out on low volume and then comes right back in on high volume on subsequent days, that's a real reason for concern** (Figures 1-10 and 1-11). You don't want to see your stock erase a decent gain entirely or fail to break out successfully and then sell off hard on big volume. My friend Dan Zanger, who was also at the 2014 Master Trader Program, said it best: "Winning horses don't back up into the gate."

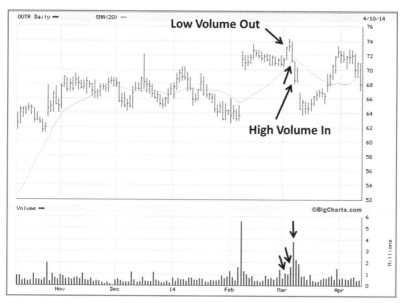

Figure 1-10 OuterWall Corp. (OUTR) 2014. The stock attempted to break out, but quickly reverses direction on an increase in volume. Low volume out, high volume in is a big red flag.

Figure 1-11 Lumber Liquidators (LL) 2013. The stock broke out of a late-stage base on low volume and failed to follow through before reversing direction and breaking hard through the 20-day and the 50-day lines on big volume—a major sell signal.

WATCH FOR MULTIPLE VIOLATIONS

Negative scenarios converging like the ones I've just described and illustrated—a low-volume breakout with no follow-through, three lower lows, and a high-volume sell-off that closes below the 20-day line—mean my expectations for this trade simply aren't being met. These violations could tip you off to impending trouble; the more violations that occur, the more likely the trade will fail. If a number of them occur, it will likely prompt me to sell, even before my stop-loss is triggered. **Depending upon how many violations occur and how severe they are, I'll either reduce my position or get out entirely. Of course, if my stop-loss is hit, then I'm out regardless!**

Depending on your strategy and your expectations, you'll be able to determine if and when your plan is being disrupted or if your expectations are materializing. The more disruptions and disappointments that occur after you buy a stock, the more you have to admit that the trade is not working out as expected and make an adjustment accordingly. Being able to admit that you've made a mistake is paramount to your success as a stock trader. Without a road map, though, how would you know how to identify a mistake?

Violations Soon After a Breakout

- Low volume out of a base—high volume back in
- Three or four lower lows without supportive action
- More down days than up days
- More bad closes than good closes
- A close below the 20-day moving average
- A close below the 50-day moving average on heavy volume
- Full retracement of a good-size gain

SQUATS AND REVERSAL RECOVERIES

While you want your stock to "behave" after your purchase, you don't want to choke off the trade unnecessarily. Just because a stock doesn't immediately take off and quickly satisfy your profit objective doesn't necessarily make the trade a failure. There are several violations like the ones I just described that will tell you if the action is ominous. Without a plan, you could miss the warning signs or flinch too quickly on a natural reaction and get stopped out prematurely. And all because you didn't develop a plan before you got into the trade.

Sometimes a stock will break out through a pivot point only to fall back into its range and close off the day's high—and then, *squat*. When this happens, I don't always jump ship and sell right away; I try to wait at least a day or two or even up to a couple of weeks to see if the stock can stage what I call a *reversal recovery* (Figures 1-12 and 1-13). This accommodation makes sense in a bull market. In some cases, it can take up to 10 days for a recovery to occur. This is not a hard-and-fast rule; some may take a little longer, while some simply fail and stop you out.

Of course, if the reversal is large enough to trigger my stop, I sell immediately, no questions asked. If the reversal causes the price to close

below its 20-day moving average on heavy volume and violations starting piling up, it lowers the probability of success and it becomes a judgment call; sometimes I sell if this happens, and sometimes I reduce my
position. If the price action tightens and volume subsides, the setup
could be improving, and it could be that you've just entered the trade
a bit early. **A *reversal recovery* means the stock was able to quickly
overcome the stalling or reversal day, and it's a positive sign.** After
you make a purchase, try to give the stock a week or two and enough
room to fluctuate normally—within the confines of your stop level, of
course. If the stock squats, don't panic; as long as your stop is not triggered and no major violations occur, wait to see if the stock can stage a
reversal recovery.

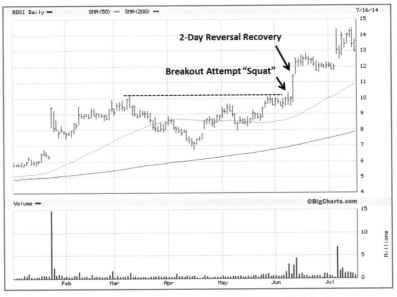

Figure 1-12   Biodelivery Science Intl. (BDSI) 2014. +80% in three
months. The stock attempted to breakout of well-formed cup-with-handle
formation, then "squatted" on the attempted breakout day. Two days later it
staged a reversal recovery. With no violations occurring and no stop hit—if
you bought on the breakout/squat day—you stay with the trade.

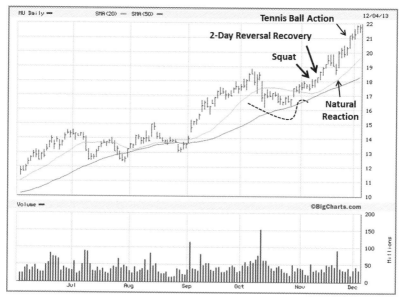

Figure 1-13   Micron Technologies (MU) 2013. +87% in 13 months. The stock attempted to emerge from a cup completion cheat (3-C) (see Section 7). The breakout stalled and closed below the midpoint of the daily range—a squat. Two days later the stock price staged a reversal recovery.

Avoid the Paralysis-Regret Cycle

All too often, investors get confused after they get into a stock and don't know what to do next. They buy and hold on for dear life, waiting for "something" to happen (meaning, they hope and pray that the stock will go their way). But without a reference point based on sound rules, they have no way to measure the action and know if things are going along as planned, or if there's real reason for concern. **All traders vacillate and struggle between two emotions: indecisiveness and regret. This inner conflict stems from not establishing a clear timeline and a solid plan up front.** The fear of regret is a powerful emotion. If you don't have a plan, you will surely experience paralyzing emotions and second-guess yourself at key decision-making moments. If you're like most traders, your emotions fluctuate constantly between two emotions and you struggle with the following:

Indecisiveness

- Should I buy?
- Should I sell?
- Should I hold?

Regret

- I should have bought
- I should have sold
- I should have held

Remember, speculation is anticipating coming movements and then waiting to be proven right or wrong. You go in with a plan and execute it. Then, after the trade is completed, you evaluate the results, troubleshoot your approach, and come back in with a new plan of attack. The key is to see things as they are—operating in the now—without seeing things as worse than they are out of fear, or better than they are out of greed. There's no sense in having a plan if you're not going to adhere to it; that would be illogical. Bottom line: If you don't have things thought out before going into a trade, then you will likely rationalize and you could be gripped with indecision at the moment you need to act swiftly.

This book is all about rules, no matter what your strategy. In other words, the rules in this book are *not* necessarily strategy-specific. And that's why this section is so important: Always go in with a plan! I'm going to show you how I apply the rules to my own trading, but whatever your approach is, if you don't have a plan, you will eventually sabotage yourself. You won't be able to manage your strategy—buy here, sell there, hold for a larger profit—unless you have a detailed blueprint that includes confirmation signals that a trade is working as expected, and violations you will heed as warnings and act accordingly.

So have a plan. Your success depends on it.

APPROACH EVERY TRADE RISK-FIRST

Every morning before the market opens I look into the mirror and say to myself, "Mark, you have the capacity to do serious damage to yourself today." Then I go to work. I do this little exercise as a way to face and acknowledge my own capacity for self-destruction and to always remember the two most important words in trading: *respect risk!*

You can't completely avoid risk, but you can minimize it and have a significant degree of control over it. **If you want to mitigate risk effectively, you simply must acknowledge that stocks don't manage themselves. You're the manager, and it's up to you to protect your hard-earned capital.** You also have to realize and confront that it's your own laziness, lack of discipline, and failure to prepare that will lead to poor performance—or even your financial demise.

With every trade I make, my approach is always "risk-first." By thinking and acting "risk-first," you know exactly what you stand to lose if you're wrong, which in trading is far more important than what you stand to gain if you're right, because if you lose all your chips, the game is over. If you get complacent and fail to respect risk, you will fail to attain big success or you will give back what you worked to attain. This I can promise you.

WHERE'S THE EXIT?

When most investors find a stock they like, all they think about is buying and how much money they're going to make. They can just taste those returns! The more they like it, the more they wished they'd bought it yesterday. Greed leads to impatience, and too often they jump in before thinking things through. "Return first," though, is not the way to big performance. To achieve superior results and survive the bear markets, you must control risk, every trade, every day. This starts with determining the stop-loss point.

With each buy order I enter, I know the exact price where I am going to sell at a loss if things don't work out as expected. I define this price level *before* **I get in.** I don't concentrate on the upside; I focus on the downside. Taking a "risk-first" approach means I understand the risk inherent in every trade and I prepare for the unthinkable. If you want big stock returns, you must consider the amount of risk you're willing to take, and have a predetermined exit plan to protect your account from a large loss. Otherwise, you will eventually give back a good portion or all of your profits and end up with only average results at best, if you're lucky.

Over the years, I have honed this discipline so that I never have to figure out what to do if the market moves against me or if there is a sudden negative development in a particular stock. I have identified the exit point *before I ever get in a trade.* That's my stop-loss, the predetermined price at which I will retreat, no questions asked. If it turns out to be a false alarm, I can always get back in. Like an insurance policy, I pay a relatively small fee to protect myself from a major loss.

Unfortunately, most investors never use stop-losses, or they try them, get stopped out, and when the stock they sold turns around and goes back up, they say, "I'm never going to do something stupid like that again." This is because they think "return first" not "risk first." **Trading without a stop-loss is like driving a car without brakes. Maybe you could make it around the block a few times, but if you did drive without brakes, how far do you think you could go before you crash?** The same holds true for trading: when you fail to trade with stop-loss protection, you are absolutely guaranteed to have a major accident; it's just a matter of time. A strong market may allow you to get away with reckless trading for a period of time, but in my experience, those who trade without a stop eventually stop trading.

RULES ARE MEANINGLESS WITHOUT DISCIPLINE

It's no good having a "mental stop"—telling yourself, *if the stock falls to "X" I will get out there*—if you don't follow it. That's like driving without ever using the brakes or, only using them on occasion. The problem with a mental stop is that it's too easy to "forget," and then hold onto a losing trade, telling yourself that you'll sell once the stock recovers. *Let me get back to breakeven and I'll get out.* The stock may keep going lower, while the loss keeps getting bigger. For most traders, it becomes even harder to sell as a loss balloons. **Every huge loss starts as a small one. The only way to protect a trade from turning into a large loss is to accept a small loss before it snowballs out of control.** In more than three decades of trading, I have not found a better way.

AVOID THE EMOTIONAL STOP-LOSS

Everyone has an "emotional stop-loss" whether they like it or not. The point at which you can't take it anymore is your emotional stop. For most investors, your emotional stop is far beyond the point that makes mathematical sense. Instead, it's a loss large enough to do significant financial as well as psychological damage. Allow enough trades to hit your emotional stop, and you will surely do damage to your confidence in addition to your capital, and as a result, you will be less likely to make sound trading decisions going forward. **I've heard some pundits say trading with a stop-loss is foolish. Only a fool would make such a statement!** I have never met a stock trader that consistently produced big returns but traded *without* some form of stop-loss protection. On the other hand, I have seen countless mediocre performers trade without it, and many of them lost it all and quit.

DON'T BECOME AN "INVOLUNTARY INVESTOR"

Investors hate to admit mistakes, so they rationalize. Amateurs fluctuate from a being a "trader" when they're right and "investor" when they are wrong. When what started out as a "trade" moves against them and starts to rack up a loss, all of a sudden they're a long-term investor. They become what Jesse Livermore called an "involuntary investor," a person who harvests a bitter crop of small profits and large losses, the exact opposite of what you want to achieve.

No one can know for sure that a stock will decline only a certain amount and then move higher. How can you tell when a 10 or 15 percent pullback is the beginning of a 50 or 60 percent decline, or worse? You can't! If you had known that your stock was going to drop, would you have bought it in the first place? Of course not!

On average, over time you will likely be correct on only 50 percent of your purchases. The best traders may pick winning stocks about 60 or 70 percent of the time in a healthy market. In fact, you can be correct on 50 percent of your stock selections and still enjoy huge success, but only if you keep your losses in check and avoid becoming an involuntary investor. You can make money by picking winning stocks only one time out of two or even three trades, but only if you sell your losers before they inflict an insurmountable toll on your account.

You must avoid rationalization, coming up with reasons and justification for why you should hold onto a losing trade. **You should always determine, in advance, the price at which you set your stop-loss. Then write it down, put it on a Post-it, and program your computer to send you an alert when that price is reached**. You can even put in a stop order with your broker that will automatically trigger when your price target is hit. The main thing is that you cut your loss immediately, without any vacillation.

Afterward, as you examine your trading results, you might decide to make some adjustments for your *next* trade. Maybe you are being stopped out too frequently because your stops are too tight. Or, your losses may be too large because your stop-losses are not tight enough. You shouldn't need to let a stock decline so far as to cause big damage before you know that you're in the wrong stock or your timing is off. If your goal is big performance, large losses are simply unacceptable and counterproductive!

How Much Risk Is Too Much?

You should definitely keep your losses to 10 percent or less, because losses work against you geometrically. As you get increasingly further away from the 10 percent mark, losses work more and more against you. A 5 percent decline takes a 5.26 percent gain to get even. With a 10 percent loss, it takes an 11 percent gain to get even. A 40 percent loss needs a 67 percent gain. After a 50 percent loss, the gain must be 100 percent. And if your position fell by 90 percent, you'd need a 900 percent gain to get even! How many stocks that you buy go up 900 percent, 100 percent, or even 67 percent? A 10 percent loss is my maximum allowance; however, my average is much less than that.

Avoid the Bucking Broncos

If a stock is highly volatile, with dramatic gyrations up and down, it's going to be a difficult issue to trade using a relatively tight stop-loss to control risk. Because of the stock's wild movements, there is a high probability that you'll get stopped out, even if the stock fluctuates normally. Setting your stops wide enough to accommodate those big swings will likely expose you to greater downside risk than you're comfortable taking or that makes mathematical sense. A risk-first approach would tell you to find another candidate. There are plenty of stocks to trade!

Think of stocks as horses in the corral. Unless you were a daredevil rodeo rider, with more broken bones than common sense, why would you pick a bucking bronco? Sure, that bronco may get from Point A to Point B, just like a volatile stock can go from $20 to $40 a share. But that end goal comes at a price. The ultimate objective is for you to stay on that horse (or in that trade) without getting bucked off (stopped out). **A stock may go from Point A to Point B, but the important question is, are *you* going to be able to stay onboard?**

What you need is a horse (stock) that can make it to the other side of the corral, but without so much volatility that you end up facedown in the dirt and trampled, right out of the gate. If you target the most volatile ones (horses and stocks), you'll go through a lot of pain and Pepto-Bismol. And, you'll feel pretty beaten up by both.

A risk-first approach is to avoid the bucking bronco that will throw you off its back at the first chance, and to focus instead on an obedient horse that takes you along for the ride. I learned that lesson many years ago, on a visit to my uncle's farm.

WHOA, THERE, BLACK ORCHID . . .

When I was 10 years old, I visited my Uncle John's horse farm, Bonnie's Acres, in Connecticut. There was a small black horse that looked perfect for a young rider like me. Except "Black Orchid" had a bad reputation for kicking and bucking. The minute I got on this mare, she took off, right toward a tree, where a low-hanging branch knocked me off and cut my face.

You'd think that would have taught me a lesson about picking which horse to ride; unfortunately, no. A few months later, when I was back at Uncle John's farm, I got on Black Orchid again. This time, she took off running and started bucking midstride. I got jostled and bounced, up and down, until Black Orchid knocked me clean off her back. Then, just to show me who was boss, she ran right over me leaving hoof prints across my back. Fortunately, I wasn't hurt too badly.

Uncle John and my cousin Dean rushed over to me. "Are you okay, Mark?" my uncle asked. I looked up at him with a dazed smile and said, "Uncle John, did you see how fast I was going?" Oh, I had speed for a short while. But I never got to the other side of the corral. Black Orchid got to the other side, but without me.

Now whenever I look at a stock, I think back to Black Orchid. Am I going to end up facedown in the dirt with hoofprints on my back, because I've decided to saddle myself to a highly volatile situation?

Stock trading doesn't have to be a nerve-wracking experience. All it takes is a good plan based on solid trading principles. Part of that plan is sacrificing trades that carry too much risk. Leave the Black Orchids in the stock market corral, and go look for a nice horse named Alpha that is capable of going the distance with you still onboard.

Backing into Risk

My stop-loss is actually an important part of my selection process. I may set my sights on a particular name, but I'm not going to buy a stock unless it offers me a low-risk entry point. You don't control risk when you sell, you control it when you buy; when you sell you simply take the loss, but the loss should already be predetermined and it should make mathematical sense. Can you afford to take a 25 percent loss if your expected gain is only 10 percent or 15 percent? If you consistently buy stocks with more reward than risk, over time you're going to be in good shape, because you will have an edge. But if you stack the odds against yourself and risk more than you stand to gain, you might as well go to a casino.

Trading Near the Danger Point

To control my risk, I want to enter my buy as close to my stop as possible. This is known as trading close to the "danger point" (Figure 2-1). Distinguishing normal behavior from abnormal is an important skill that you should spend time developing. Buying breakouts and setting stops based on a percentage drop is a good start and will likely put you ahead of most traders. However, the really great traders know how to discern proper price action from dangerous price action, and they place trades close to the point at which a stock flashes warnings and the trade sours.

The goal for optimal stop-loss placement is to set it at a level that will allow the stock price enough room for normal fluctuation, but close enough to the danger point that's not too much risk mathematically. Smart traders set stops based on the underlying technical action in line with the reality of their own prevailing arithmetic. Trading near the danger point means trading low-risk entries.

Figure 2-1   Medivation (MDVN) 2012. +112% in seven months. The stock broke out of a tight range and then pulled back near the breakout point or danger level.

KNOW WHAT YOU CONTROL

When risk is involved, it's human nature to want to control everything. In trading (as in many things in life) there are only a few things over which you have control. In fact, there are only four things in trading that you can control directly. Before you make the trade, you control:

- What you buy
- How much you buy
- When you buy

After you make the trade, you control:

- When you sell

That's it—three decisions prior to making the trade, and only one to make after you're in the trade. Once you own a stock, you can't control whether it goes up or down, any more than you can influence the weather. The stock, just like the weather, is going to do whatever it's going to do.

You do your research, take your position, and hope to have success based on your criteria.

But what if things don't work out as you hoped? Knowing what you control will help you keep things in perspective and focus your attention and energy on what you can do to manage your risk. With only one decision that you have direct control over after you're in a trade (when you sell), imagine how important that decision must be.

WHO'S RIGHT AND WHO CAN BE WRONG

Making the decision to cut your loss in a stock requires that you accept the notion that *only you* can be wrong; the market is never wrong. This is a very difficult reality for most traders to accept because of the ego. We all have egos, but when the ego drives your investment decisions, the end result is rarely a good one. **The ego is 100 percent responsible for you stubbornly digging in, holding onto losses, and not being able to admit your mistakes.** The ego drives rationalization; "I'm in a good company that's not going to go out of business, I'm not selling."

Personally, I'm not in the stock market to claim victory that I found a company that won't go out of business. I'm looking for stocks that make big and fast price gains. The ego hurts investors time and time again. If you don't believe that the ego is assertively at work in your trading, consider the following:

- Scenario A. You bought a stock, and soon after it started selling off, you cut your loss and took a $2,500 hit. The next day the stock soared and you would have made $25,000 on the trade. **How do you feel?**
- Scenario B. You bought a stock, and soon after it started selling off, you cut your loss and took a $2,500 hit. The next day the stock gapped down on the open and plummeted; had you stayed in the trade and not cut your loss, you would have lost $25,000. **Now, how do you feel?**

In both scenarios, you have the same $2,500 loss.

I'll sell when I get back to even. Does that sound familiar? You bought a stock at $35 a share and were reluctant to sell when it fell to $32. The stock then sank to $26, and you would have been delighted to have the opportunity to sell it at $32 again. When the stock then sank to $16, you asked yourself, why didn't I sell it at $32 or even $26 when I had the chance to get out with a relatively small loss? The reason investors get into this situation is that they lack a sound plan for dealing with risk and allow their egos to get involved.

A strategy is only as good as your willingness to follow your own rules. A sound plan takes implementation, which takes discipline. That part I cannot do for you. It's your ego that doesn't want to be wrong, and it's the pain association you have with "wrong" that creates the problem. To fix this, you need to associate pleasure with small losses and pain with large losses. This will help you emotionally take a small loss before it becomes a large one.

Trading Lessons

The market is a demanding taskmaster. Make a mistake and you will get penalized, not only financially but emotionally. The market can mug your pocket and beat up on your psyche. Coming back from losses in dollars and self-confidence is not easy. But there are ways of protecting yourself, which work with any strategy, starting with the first two rules: *always go in with a plan* and *approach every trade risk-first*.

If you can't abide by these foundational rules—let alone the rules that follow—you'll have to take a hard look at yourself. What exactly are you trying to accomplish? Do you want to make money, or are you engaged in an exercise in ego to prove that, somehow, you know more than the market? Or are you engaged in an exercise in self-destruction? Most of us know people who, sadly, have such a poor self-image that they think they don't deserve good things, and so they sabotage their own chances of success. Yes, you deserve success! But only if you do the right things; the market has no pity on fools.

Trading is one of the most potent litmus tests for showing what you're made of. You'll find out, and fairly quickly, if you are capable of doing what's required, emotionally and physically. If you are unwilling to make the right choices, that lesson is likely to be a painful one.

My rules are meant to be used as a playbook that can be adapted to any strategy, the fundamental building blocks of a successful trading plan. The great football coach Vince Lombardi focused on fundamentals, making sure his team could block, tackle, run, catch, and pass better than anybody else. He knew that doing the basics better than everyone else was how games were won.

The stock market is a great way to increase your wealth, and if you're disciplined, your chances of success are very good. However, before you start thinking about the cars and boats you're going to buy with the profits, you'd first better think about how you will avoid losing your principal. **Not losing big is the single most important factor for winning big. As a speculator, losing is not a choice, but how much you lose is.** You're going to make many mistakes; we all make mistakes. A mistake isn't a problem when we acknowledge it, deal with it, and learn from it. But, when we dig in and refuse to budge, that's when it all goes down the drain and little problems turn into big problems. This is true in trading and in life.

Long-term success in the stock market has nothing to do with hope or luck. Winning stock traders have rules and a well-thought-out plan. Conversely, losers lack rules, or if they have rules, they don't stick to them for very long; they deviate.

Remember, always trade risk-first. This is the key rule that keeps you in the game, playing long after the undisciplined, uninitiated, and unfocused are forced to the sidelines or driven to the poorhouse.

NEVER RISK MORE THAN YOU EXPECT TO GAIN

With a flip of a coin you will be wrong just as often as you're right, 50/50. But what if you could win two dollars on heads and only lose one dollar on tails? With those odds, you would want to flip that coin as many times as possible, wouldn't you? Let's assume that you decide to limit your losses to 10 percent maximum, because after that point the losses mathematically begin to work against you; the more you descend the loss ladder, the worse it gets. The question now is, have you adequately controlled your risk? Some traders would probably say yes, that limiting losses at a maximum of 10 percent sounds about right.

But how can they know? More to the point, how can *you* know where you should limit *your* losses if you only look at one side of the equation? **In order to set an appropriate stop-loss, you need to know your average gain, not just what you *hope* to make on each individual trade, but a number you can reasonably expect to occur over time on average.**

You need actual numbers in order to accurately establish your risk versus your potential reward. Here's why: Suppose that while you are risking 10 percent on the downside, your profitable trades average only about a 5 percent gain. Do you really want to risk 10 percent to make 5 percent? You would need to be correct on almost 70 percent of your trades to just break even. But let's say you average 10 percent on your winners and you only risk 5 percent. Now you can be right on only one out of three trades and still not get in any real trouble.

Your Batting Average

Risk is not an arbitrary number. The amount you risk must be adjusted based on the amount you stand to gain. Therefore, losses are a function of expected gain. Although I infrequently get an outsized loss that goes much beyond my average parameters, I rarely take a loss larger than 8 to 10 percent. On average, my losses are about half of that. Now let's assume that, on average, my gains run about 15 percent. With these percentages—4 to 5 percent losses and 15 percent gains, on average—it appears I'm keeping my risk in line. To know for sure, though, I need one more number: the batting average.

As every baseball fan knows, nobody bats a thousand; even batting .500 is an impossibility. Ted Williams, who was considered the greatest hitter of all time, batted just over .400 in his best season; his career average was .344. Admittedly, baseball isn't trading, but it does give some perspective on the fact that even people who excel in their fields do not have a perfect track record. Trading certainly follows that truth.

In trading, your batting average is simply your percentage of winning trades (PWT). Although your batting average is not something you have direct control over—like cutting a loss—other than how well you choose what stocks to buy and when to buy and sell them, it's an important number and part of the calculation that will determine how much risk you should take. **To determine the appropriate percentage to risk, you need to make sure your losses are contained as a factor of your gains, because you never want to risk more than you stand to win.**

At a 50 percent batting average, you're right as many times as you're wrong, so to maintain a 2:1 reward/risk ratio, you need to keep your losses to half of your gains. However, at a 40 percent batting average, in order to maintain the same 2:1 reward/risk ratio, your losses will have to be contained to one-third the level of your gains. For example:

- 50 percent batting average
- 10 percent average gain
- 5 percent average loss

$$50*10/50*5 = 2{:}1$$

- 40 percent batting average
- 15 percent average gain
- 5 percent average loss

$$40*15/60*5 = 2{:}1$$

Building in "Failure"

Most people are surprised when I tell them I would rather be able to maintain profitability at a 25 percent batting average than a 75 percent batting average. Why? Because it allows me to be wrong many times and still make money; it builds "failure" into the system. I try to build as much failure as possible into my trading in the areas that I don't have direct control over. You can't control your batting average because you can't control what a stock does after you buy it. My way of governing the areas that I don't directly control is not to rely on them too heavily. My edge is maintained by keeping my losses at a fraction of my gains. **The smaller I keep my losses in relation to my gains, the more batting average risk I can tolerate, which means the more times I can be wrong and still make money.**

The Science of Volatility and Expectancy

You may have heard that when setting a stop-loss you should allow more room for volatile price action; you should widen your stops on the basis of the volatility of the underlying stock. I strongly disagree. Most often, high volatility is experienced during a tough market environment. During difficult periods, your gains will be smaller than normal, and your percentage of profitable trades (your batting average) will definitely be lower than usual; so your losses must be cut shorter to compensate. It would be fair to assume that in difficult trading periods your batting average is likely to fall below 50 percent. **Once your batting average drops below 50 per-**

cent, increasing your risk proportionately to your gains will eventually cause you to hit negative expectancy; the more your batting average drops, the sooner negative expectancy will be realized.

A popular indicator that is used to set a stop-loss level is the Average True Range or ATR. It's a measure of volatility introduced by Welles Wilder. Mr. Wilder originally developed the ATR for commodities, but the indicator is also used for stocks and indexes. Simply put, a stock experiencing a high level of volatility will have a higher ATR or wider stop, and a low-volatility stock will have a lower ATR or tighter stop. I am not a fan of the concept of adjusting for volatility by widening your stop. Just because your gains are larger than your losses doesn't necessarily mean that you will make money, even if your wins are twice as large as your losses.

Let me illustrate: At a 40 percent batting average, you make more money with 4 percent profits than with 42 percent profits (10 times more), assuming you maintain the same 2:1 reward/risk ratio. This may sound hard to believe, but it's true. Why? Because losses work geometrically against you. Once you understand this, you will learn one of the great secrets to profitable trading. Do the math!

- 40 percent batting average
- 4 percent average gain
- 2 percent average loss
- **Gain/loss ratio 2:1**

This results in a net *profit* of 3.63 percent in 10 trades.

- 40 percent batting average
- 42 percent average gain
- 21 percent average loss
- **Gain/loss ratio: 2:1**

This results in a net *loss* of 1.16 percent in 10 trades.

NOT ALL RATIOS ARE CREATED EQUAL

At a 40 percent batting average, your optimal gain/loss ratio is 20 percent/10 percent; at this ratio your return on investment (ROI) over 10 trades is 10.20 percent. Thereafter, with increasing losses in proportion to your gains, the return actually declines. Armed with this knowledge, you can understand which ratio, given a particular batting average, will yield the best expected return. This illustrates the power of finding the optimal ratio. Any less and you make less money; however, any more and you also make less money.

If your winning trades were to more than double from 20 percent gains to 42 percent gains and you maintained a 2:1 gain/loss ratio by cutting your losses at 21 percent instead of 10 percent, you would actually lose money. You're still maintaining the same ratio, so how could you be losing? This is the dangerous nature of losses; they work geometrically against you. At a 50 percent batting average, if you made 100 percent on your winners and lost 50 percent on your losers, you would do nothing but break even. You would make more money taking profits at 4 percent and cutting your losses at 2 percent. Not surprisingly, as your batting average drops, it gets much worse. At a 30 percent batting average, profiting 100 percent on your winners and giving back 50 percent on your losers, you would have a whopping 93.75 percent loss in just 10 trades (Figure 3-1).

10 Trade Compounded Return on Investment (ROI)

% Gain	% Loss	G/L Ratio	@ 30% Bat. Avg.	@ 40% Bat. Avg.	@ 50% Bat. Avg.
4.00%	2.00%	2:1	-2.35%	3.63%	10.00%
6.00%	3.00%	2:1	-3.77%	5.16%	14.92%
8.00%	4.00%	2:1	-5.34%	6.49%	19.80%
12.00%	6.00%	2:1	-8.89%	8.55%	29.34%
14.00%	7.00%	2:1	-10.86%	9.27%	33.95%
16.00%	8.00%	2:1	-12.93%	9.79%	38.43%
20.00%	10.00%	2:1	-17.35%	**10.20%**	46.93%
24.00%	12.00%	2:1	-22.08%	9.80%	54.71%
30.00%	15.00%	2:1	-29.57%	7.71%	64.75%
36.00%	18.00%	2:1	-37.23%	4.00%	72.49%
42.00%	21.00%	2:1	-45.01%	-1.16%	77.66%
48.00%	24.00%	2:1	-52.52%	-7.55%	**80.04%**
54.00%	27.00%	2:1	-59.65%	-14.88%	79.56%
60.00%	30.00%	2:1	-66.27%	-22.90%	76.23%
70.00%	35.00%	2:1	-75.92%	-37.01%	64.75%
80.00%	40.00%	2:1	-83.67%	-51.02%	46.93%
90.00%	45.00%	2:1	-89.56%	-63.93%	24.62%
100.00%	50.00%	2:1	-93.75%	-75.00%	0.00%

Figure 3-1   At a 40 percent batting average, the optimal gain/loss ratio is 20 percent/10 percent; any higher or lower and you make less money. At a 50 percent batting average, the optimal reward to risk shifts up to 48 percent/24 percent.

REAL-LIFE APPLICATION

If you're trading poorly and your batting average falls below the 50 percent level, the last thing you want to do is increase the room you give your stocks on the downside. This is not an opinion; it's a mathematical fact. Many investors give their losing positions more freedom, and as a result inflict much deeper losses. Their results begin to slip, and they get knocked out of a handful of trades; then they watch the stocks they sold at a loss turn around and go back up. What do they say to themselves? "Maybe I should have given the stock more room to fluctuate; I'd still be in it." This is just the opposite of what you should do.

The only time I give my stock positions more room to fluctuate is when things are working well, then I may be a little more forgiving because a good market will tend to bail me out from time to time. Conversely, in a difficult market environment, profits will be smaller than normal and losses will be larger; downside gaps will be more common, and you will likely experience greater slippage. The smart way to handle this is to do the following:

- Tighten up stop-losses. If you normally cut losses at 7 to 8 percent, cut them at 5 to 6 percent.
- Settle for smaller profits. If you normally take profits of 15 to 20 percent on average, take profits at 10 to 12 percent.
- If you're trading with the use of leverage, get off margin immediately.
- Reduce your exposure with regard to your position sizes as well as your overall capital commitment.
- Once you see your batting average and reward/risk profile improve, you can start to extend your parameters gradually back to normal levels.

THE "HOLY GRAIL"

There is no certainty when speculating in the stock market—that's why it's called speculation. Therefore, speculation is based on certain assumptions. When you buy a stock, you are hoping that others will soon perceive value in the stock and buy the shares, creating demand that moves the price higher.

Managing your reward/risk ratio requires relying on assumptions: What amount of reward can you expect versus the level of risk you are taking? Assuming you're a 50/50 trader, if you are cutting losses at, say, 10 percent, with the assumption that your winners will rise 20 percent on average, but your upside turns out to be only 8 percent—and not the 20 percent that you anticipated—you are obviously going to lose money over time because you have a negative expectancy.

Expectancy is your percentage of winning trades multiplied by your average gain, divided by your percentage of losing trades multiplied by your average loss. Maintain a positive expectancy, and you're a winner. **My results went from average to stellar when I finally made the choice that I was going to make every trade an intelligent risk/reward decision.** The following formula is the only holy grail I know of:

PWT (percentage of winning trades)*AG (average gain) /
PLT (percentage of losing trades)*AL (average loss) = Expectancy

How to Set Your Expectations

As we discussed, your risk needs to be determined as a function of your expected profits; losses are a function of expected gain. Determining your upside potential can be accomplished in one of two ways. One way is to use Theoretical Base Assumptions (TBA). Let's say you foresee a big run in a stock—a 50 percent move. Or maybe your expectations are somewhat more modest, with a projected 20 percent gain. These numbers sound great; but is it realistic to assume that (A) the move will actually materialize and (B) you will be able to capture it? The problem with the TBA approach is that there is no real-life evidence that you will realize these expectations. Have you in fact been accomplishing this level of profitability consistently?

You pick a stock that's trading at, say, $30 a share, believing that it will run up to its old high at $34.50, which would be a 15 percent gain. You want your potential reward to be three times the risk, so you put a stop in at $28.50—5 percent below your purchase price. This approach is based solely on a theoretical assumption: What you think should happen based on your technical analysis of the stock, the way the planets are lining up, or some other reason you believe a stock can reach a particular level. You may reach your target, or you may not. No matter how good your assumptions are, theoretical results are not based on reality, and they do not account for human error. Furthermore, emotions can cause you to override your own system.

If you use TBA alone, I can almost guarantee that there will be a big gap between your assumptions and the truth of your results. It is better to deal with reality than mere projections.

The Result-Based Assumption

The second way to determine your expectations is to use what I call a Result-Based Assumption (RBA). This means examining what you've gained, on average, on your actual trades. Let's say that, over the past year, you've averaged 10 percent profits on your winning trades, and you've been profitable on half of your commitments. Can you afford to take a 10 percent loss? No, because you have no edge (based on what you generally produce in profits). You need to limit your risk to a smaller percentage, such as 5 percent. Or, if your average gain is only 4 percent, you will need to cut your losses at maybe 2 percent, which might be okay for a day trader. Using RBA, the amount of risk that you take is directly correlated with the actual results you and your strategy produced; if you want to reap twice or three times the reward for the amount of risk, then you would determine that risk based on your own closed trades.

Using RBA to determine your risk takes discipline. Most traders set their stops based on the crystal ball assumption: what they want to occur. For example, let's say you believe a stock has the potential for a 40 percent return. Since you are a 2R trader—winning 2 units for each unit risked—you tell yourself you can set your stop at 20 percent below where you're getting in the market. Wrong! Your actual results show an average 10 percent gain. Your stop placement should consider those results, especially if they vastly differ from your theoretical-based assumption.

Over time, as your *actual* performance improves, you can adjust your stop accordingly. However, if your results worsen, you have to tighten your risk. You might be able to make really good assumptions and your theoretical assumption on one trade or several trades may be excellent, and even work out as expected. But your performance is going to be driven by the results that you are producing over time *on average*. **Your actual results encompass not only your strategy, but more important, your foibles, idiosyncrasies, and emotions that often override a portion of even the best laid-out plans.**

Whatever your strategies, whether you hold your position for an hour or several months, know your results and do the math. Based on that reality, set your expectations for the next trade you make. Think of your average gain as a pace car that you ride behind, maintaining a certain distance.

USING STAGGERED STOPS

You don't necessarily have to set your stop-loss on your entire position at one price. You can use what I call staggered or bracketed stops and still mitigate losses at your desired level, but have a better chance at maintaining at least a portion of your position in the stock should it move against you. If you want to limit your risk at say 5 percent, you can set a 5 percent stop, and if it hits that level, you're out. Or, a more conservative approach would be to set a stop on one-third at a 3 percent loss, one-third at 5 percent, and one-third at 8 percent. Your total loss would still be around 5 percent, but it would give you a chance to stay in two-thirds of the position above a 5 percent loss and maintain one-third of the position down to an 8 percent stop.

In the early stages of a new bull market, a new emerging leader could make a huge price move. If you give the stock more room on a portion of the shares, even a small position in a big mover could make a big difference in your bottom line. The key to using staggered stops is to try to maintain your line without getting knocked out of the entire position.

I like to use staggered stops when I think a stock has a chance of making a really big gain and I want to have the best chance possible to stay in the position. When market volatility is high and my stops are getting hit, I sometimes bracket my stops to have a chance at staying in two-thirds of the position at my original stop.

Staggered Stops

Bracket $\left\{\begin{array}{l} \text{1/3 @ 4 percent} \\ \textbf{1/3 @ 6 percent} \\ \text{1/3 @ 8 percent} \end{array}\right.$

Total Loss 6 percent

Figure 3-2 Staggering stops starts with establishing a level of risk and then bracketing around it.

In Figure 3-3, the amount I'm willing to lose on the trade is 6 percent. But I decided to play it a bit safe and bracket my stops around that num-

Figure 3-3 Isis Pharmaceuticals (ISIS) 2014. +54% in two months. The stock pulled back 6.10 percent, stopping you out completely if you used a 6 percent stop. By bracketing stops, selling half at 4 percent and half at 8 percent, you maintained 6 percent risk, but stayed in half the position.

ber. Using a 4 percent stop on half the position and an 8 percent stop on the remaining half allows the stock a couple more percent to fluctuate on half the position. My total loss on the trade is still 6 percent. You can also do this with cutting your stop into three trades or whatever combination you desire.

When Should You Raise Your Stop?

I have some general guidelines as to when I raise my stop above the initial placement. Any stock that rises to a multiple of my stop-loss and is above my average gain should never be allowed to go into the loss column. When the price of a stock I own rises by three times my risk and my gain is higher than my average, I almost always move my stop up to at least breakeven.

Suppose I buy a stock at $50 and decide that I'm willing to risk 5 percent on the trade ($47.50 stop for a $2.50 risk). If the stock advances to $57.50 ($7.50 profit = 3 × $2.50), I move my stop to at least $50. If the stock continues to rise, I start to look for an opportunity to sell on the way up and nail down all or at least some of my profit. If I get stopped out at breakeven, I still have my capital—nothing gained but nothing lost. **You may feel dumb breaking even on a trade that was once at a profit; however, you'll feel a lot worse if you turn a good-size gain into a loser.** I am also inclined to move my stop up after the stock price experiences a natural reaction and then recovers to a new high.

Move your stop up when your stock rises by two or three times your risk, particularly if that number is above your historical average gain (Figure 3-4). This will help guard you against losses, protecting your capital and your confidence.

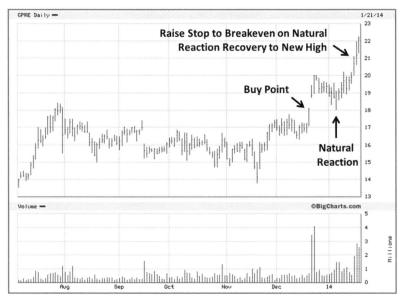

Figure 3-4   Green Plains (GPRE) 2014. +150% in eight months. The stock broke out and then experienced a natural reaction. The price then moved into new high ground, taking out the natural reaction high and attaining a decent profit. That's a good time to raise your stop.

ADDING EXPOSURE WITHOUT ADDING RISK

I like to try and make as much as I can on a winning stock position. As a result, I get creative with the ways I pyramid and add to positions. My goal, as always, is to minimize risk and maximize my potential gains. Here's how I apply a trade management technique I call the Add and Reduce.

In the example in Figure 3-5, I buy 1,000 shares of a stock at $16.50 and set a stop at $15.50, a $1 loss. This means I own 1,000 shares with $1,000 of risk. The stock then rallies and sets a new buy point. I then add an additional 1,000 shares as the stock moves through the new buy point at $17.50, and then set a $1 stop on the entire 2,000 shares at $16.50, doubling my size while keeping the same $1,000 risk. What I'm doing is letting my profits finance additional risk. If my second buy was at $18.50 with the same $1 stop, I would be doubling my size with zero risk of principal. This is how I keep my drawdowns low and make big returns by scaling into positions.

The Add and Reduce
Averaging Up without Adding Risk

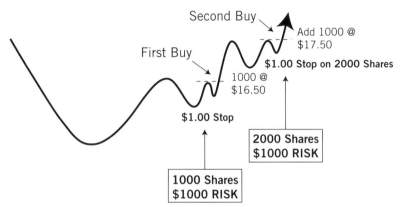

Figure 3-5   Pyramiding technique uses paper profit to finance a scaled-up trade while keeping dollar risk constant.

ALWAYS PLAY PERCENTAGE BALL

> The public . . . demands certainties; it must be told definitely
> . . . that this is true and that is false! But there are no certainties.
>
> —*H. L. Mencken*

Professional baseball players talk about playing "percentage ball." With the score 1–0 in the third inning and a man on first base, percentage ball dictates that the next batter will bunt. He will probably be thrown out at first base, but he will advance the other runner to second base, putting him in a position to score the tying run. Here, the professional thing to do is to "play it safe" to try merely to even the score. In a more desperate situation, percentage ball may call for the hit and run, home run, or some other long-chance play.

Calculating risks shrewdly is the main ingredient for consistent superior performance. **Pros play percentage ball, and that's why, in the long run, they are more consistent than amateurs. Therefore, it could be said that the difference between an amateur and a pro lies in consistency.** Relying on the probabilities based on a positive mathematical expectation to win (your "edge") will lead to success. The more times you turn over your edge, the more profit you will make, and the more likely that the probabilities will distribute correctly—representative of the true probabilities—over time.

Professionals understand that stock trading is not dictated by absolutes or certainties; they make decisions based on probabilities. They choose the course of action that seems to offer the highest percentage for success in the current moment. As a stock trader, you shouldn't hope for perfect answers to everything; as with most things, there are none. You can only accept or reject the wisdom of playing percentage ball.

WAIT FOR PREMIUM HANDS

Imagine you're in a game of Texas Hold'em and you're dealt a pair of aces. If you go all-in with your money before the flop, you have an 80 percent chance of winning heads-up. Now, let's say you follow that strategy, but you don't win because another player draws out and makes a higher hand to the river. Does that mean that the next time you have a pair of aces you'll say, "Oh, I'm never going to bet on them again"? Of course you'll bet on the aces, because those are the best two cards in poker; it's a premium hand. It doesn't mean you will win every time with that hand. Knowing the mathematical probability, however, you know that 8 times out of 10, a pair of aces will be the winning hand.

Your results in poker and in the stock market are all about what happens over time—not the flukes and outliers. Your goal is to place trades with the best chances of success at the lowest possible risk. If you apply sound rules, your preparation and criteria will increase your probability of success. And if it doesn't work out, then remember: it's better to lose correctly than to win incorrectly. Losing correctly can lead you to a fortune, because you are only a short-term loser; but because of your discipline and mathematical edge, you're a winner over time, and you will be able to compound those wins. On the other hand, winning incorrectly only reinforces bad habits that ultimately fail, and could very well lead you to bankruptcy.

That, in a nutshell, is the difference between gambling and investing. With gambling, the odds are against you, and you will definitely lose over time. With investing, if you follow the right rules, you will achieve success and win over time because you have a positive mathematical edge or expectancy. But you must not risk more than you can reasonably expect to gain; otherwise, you're stacking the odds against you, and that's gambling.

WHY MOST INVESTORS FAIL TO LIMIT THEIR RISK

Investors often become emotionally attached to their stock holdings. When their stock takes a dive, it's a blow to their trader's ego. This, in turn, leads to excuses and rationalizing why they should not sell. **The reason most investors fail to sell and cut their loss short is because they fear that after they sell the stock might go back up and they will be wrong twice. It's driven by the fear of regret, which stems from pure ego!** Ironically, the same fear grips investors when they have a profit and feel pressured to sell too quickly. Why? Because they fear if they don't sell the stock may go down and erase their gain.

To be successful at trading, your vanity must take a backseat, and you must remove emotion—hope, fear, and pride have no place in a trading plan. You simply cannot afford to allow your need to be right to override good judgment. It's a false truth. You are not going to be correct all of the time, and you are going to have losses. In fact, you are probably only going to be correct about 50 percent of the time, and that's if you're good. It's how you handle when you're wrong that will determine your ultimate success.

In trading and in life, how you deal with losing is the difference between mediocrity and greatness. Remember, losses are a function of expected gain. The key is to keep your losses less than your gains; always think risk versus reward and base your risk on the reality of your trading results. If you can get a reasonable idea of what your gains will be and how often you can expect them to occur, the stop-loss simply becomes a mathematical equation. But the key is to remember not to risk more than you expect to gain.

KNOW THE TRUTH ABOUT YOUR TRADING

A medical research worker, testing the effect of a new drug on cancer in chickens, was overjoyed to find that it seemed to cure in a high percentage of cases. Word of his success quickly spread and he was invited to address a medical convention. In his talk, he described the drug, his techniques, and finally his results. These he reported as follows: "An amazingly high percentage of the chickens, one-third of them showed a complete cure. In another third, there seemed to be no effect . . . and, the other chicken ran away."

—*Burton P. Fabricand*

THE SCIENCE OF WINNING

Many years ago, I became a slot car racing enthusiast. For those of you who aren't familiar with it, a slot car is an electric-powered miniature vehicle that races on an eight-lane track. A toy, but taken pretty seriously in some circles. There are even slot car competitions, pitting the fastest cars and the most skilled "drivers" against each other. At the track where I raced on weekends, I became acquainted with a man everyone called Rocky, who was a local legend in the slot car circle; he had even won a national championship. In time, he and I became close friends.

A few years later, during a dinner after I had just won a local competition, Rocky told a story about the first time he saw me at the slot car track. He said, "I knew when I saw him with a stopwatch and a notebook he meant business. Seeing that, I knew he came to win."

I stumbled upon slot car racing as I was walking through an outdoor strip mall. I looked through the window of a local track and thought to myself, *Wow that looks like fun*. So, I went in and rented a slot car and was instantly hooked. Prior to that day, I had never seen a slot car in my life, so I had to learn by trial and error. I immediately bought a bunch of equipment and started racing slot cars. I was challenged by the track's clock that measured lap times. I wanted to know what would help me get faster times. So, I would do 20 laps and change the tires, and then do another 20 laps and try cutting the tires down. Then I would try a different motor or body style and do another 20 laps. With every lap, I carefully documented the results in a notebook. I made all sorts of adjustments and then logged the times to record the effects.

Slot car racing was only a hobby for me, but I approached it the same way I did everything else: I kept track of my results, paying as much attention to when something went wrong as when everything was right. Unless I measured my results, how could I identify my mistakes and know where and how to improve? How else could I learn what was working and what was counterproductive?

Whether you're talking about perfecting slot car racing or stock trading, the power of measurement is an invaluable tool for those who have the discipline to use it routinely. **By keeping track of your results, you will gain insight into yourself and your trading that no book, seminar, indicator, or system could ever tell you.** Your results are the fingerprints of everything you do, from your criteria for identifying trades to your ability and consistency in executing them. Your results are your personal truth.

In business they say, "What gets measured gets managed." In trading, however, many times things go unmeasured. Many people don't know what or how to measure their results or they think it's unnecessary. Most simply don't understand how to use the information and apply it in a practical way to improve their trading. I'm going to show you how.

FIRST GET YOUR HEAD OUT OF THE SAND

At my Master Trader Program Workshops, I always ask for a show of hands of how many people know their average gain, average loss, and percentage of winning trades. In every seminar I've given over the years, I never get more than a few hands. The vast majority attest to the sad truth: few traders know the truth about their trading!

Think about that for a moment: If you don't know your own trading results, how can you intelligently set expectations? It's like flying a plane without an instrument panel; how would you know if you're level? If you don't know the kind of gains you're making, how will you know how much you should risk? You might as well sling darts at a dartboard—blindfolded!

Few individuals go beyond the buying and selling of stocks based on gut feeling, rumors, tips, or news stories. Even fewer put in place a disciplined approach for measuring the key aspects of their *trading results*, which is crucial for arriving at reasonable assumptions and achieving consistent trading success. The fact is, measuring results is not very popular because most people don't like to look at their bad trades; they choose to just forget about them as if they are going to magically improve with little effort and study. This is lazy and a big mistake. The first step to success in the stock market is to get your head out of the sand, and that starts with post-analysis of your results. The most valuable information about your trading is *your trading*!

KEEPING YOURSELF HONEST

It's a fact of life in the stock market: what you think should happen very rarely materializes perfectly. Those rose-colored glasses can skew your view of your own trading results. That is, unless you keep things in perspective and keep yourself honest.

Whether you're a new trader just starting out in the market or you've been at it for a while, you should definitely keep a spreadsheet of your results—every trade (and not just the trades you want to remember). Record where you bought and where you sold every single trade. Pretty soon you'll have a track record of average losses and average wins, and the frequency of the wins and losses. I also keep track of my largest gain and largest loss each month, as well as my average holding time for all my gains and losses.

As you collect this data and calculate your numbers, don't mix strategies. If you were a day trader for a few months, and then switched to swing trading or to long-term investing, you don't want to compute an average across all those results. Keep your records strategy-specific. This way you can control the risk/reward ratio for each trade, not letting your losses get larger than "x" percent, because you're only gaining "y" percent, with a frequency of "z" percent.

This is precisely what insurance companies do, with an actuarial approach to projecting the life expectancy of people grouped together by certain demographics and other factors, such as age, lifestyle, and health status. After analyzing all the characteristics of the group, the insurance company knows that, on average, life expectancy for this group of people will be, say, 77 years old. Given the current age of the person, the insurance company can project how many years before it will likely pay a death benefit payment. It can then establish the amount of premium to be collected over time to cover the death benefit and make a profit.

Of course, the insurance company can't be absolutely sure that every person in that group will die at 77, just as you won't know the precise amount of profit of any one of your winners. However, insurers have mastered the science of making actuarial projections based on where the bulk of the data aligns.

Think of your trades the same way, using real data. Certain events will stick out: like that 60 percent return you made on a trade that jumped up on a buyout. But determining your risk based on your best trade provides no protection. **Your average gain is the important figure to base your risk on; you should know this number. That's the best way to determine how much risk you should take per trade.** Just as insurance companies adjust premiums to account for life expectancy, you can adjust your stop-loss to account for the life expectancy of your gains—where they tend to expire on average. If your gains average 15 percent and you want to maintain a 2:1 reward/risk ratio, then your stop would need to be set at no more than 7.5 percent.

Log a Journal

I always insisted that anyone who worked for me never show up to a meeting without a pad and pen. It was mandatory that everyone take accurate notes and keep a journal. **People who think they can remember even a fraction of what they hear and see in any one day are arrogant and delusional. You must write things down!** When you go to hear someone speak, record it (if allowed) or take a lot of notes. Same goes for your trading. You should keep a daily journal and commit to updating it regularly without fail. I've made it a habit to have a pen, a pad, and a digital recorder on me always. This is one of the surest ways to determine immediately if someone really wants to be a winner.

A few years ago, I met with a young man who was getting involved in the stock market. When we went out to dinner together, he started asking me questions about stocks. As I started to answer his question, he stopped me. "Hold on one second," he said and whipped out a little pad and a pen. "Okay, continue." As I started talking, this lad wrote down every word I said. I thought to myself, *this kid is going to be a winner*. He wasn't neglecting one piece of information.

Winners don't take things for granted. They realize that every experience good or bad is a precious gold nugget, a lesson that should be studied and built upon. They realize the limitation of only committing things to memory. They are always prepared, and they keep a journal they can reflect upon and compare expectations to reality.

LET THE SPREADSHEET MAKE
ITS WAY INTO YOUR TRADING

Your spreadsheet is more than just a record of past performance to tuck away or glance at every now and then. It is the precise guide for handling your next trades. When you are cognizant of your numbers, you will weigh the impact of every trade against your own records. Your stats will literally make their way into your trading and guide you. For example, a stock moves against you, from a 5 percent loss to 8 percent and then 10 percent. Suddenly, a bell goes off in your head: You're going to have to log that loss in your spreadsheet and look at it (and its impact on your average) every time you examine your numbers. Not only is a larger average loss going to hurt your performance, but you will need bigger gains in the future to offset it. Before that happens, with your spreadsheet in mind, cut your losses before they reach the maximum level. **Every time I'm about to make a trading decision, I ask myself,** *how is this going to look on my spreadsheet?*

On the flip side, let's say you're at a gain. The stock shoots up quickly, rising 15 percent and keeps moving, until it's up 20, 25, and then 30 percent. Your win is now three times your historical average of say 10 percent. As greed starts to take over, you wonder, *how high can this go?* This is precisely when you need to let the spreadsheet make its way into your trading and be mindful of the reality of your own math. Logging a 30 percent gain would do wonders for your average win column. Given that prospect, you wouldn't want to let your profits slip back to 10 percent, or even worse, lower.

THE TRADING TRIANGLE

In photography, one of my newfound passions, the three variables are ISO ("film speed" or sensitivity to light), the f-stop (the size of the camera aperture to let in light), and the shutter speed (how fast the shutter "clicks"). This "triangle" of factors determines the exposure. These three dynamics (the sides of the triangle) will affect whether the picture will be under- or overexposed. You will need to adjust them in relation to each other so that you get the optimal exposure for the visual effect you're going for.

In trading, we can think of the triangle in much the same way. Instead of ISO, f-stop, and shutter speed, the three legs of the trading triangle (Figure 4-1) are:

- Your average win size: how much do you win, on a percentage basis, across all your winning trades?
- Your average loss size: how much do you lose, on a percentage basis, across all your losing trades?
- Your ratio of wins to losses: your percentage of winning trades, or what is referred to as your "batting average."

You need to start with the *reality* of your actual trading results in order to maintain an edge or mathematical advantage in any given trade. Each leg of the trading triangle will show you where you need to put your focus in order to maintain that edge. For example, if your batting average is .500 (half wins and half losses) and your average loss is say 6 percent, that's not bad. But if you find that your average gain is only 5 percent, to be profitable you will need to either make more on your winning trades, win more often, or tighten up your stop and lose less on your losing trades.

Figure 4-1 By balancing the trading triangle to arrive at a positive mathematical expectation or edge, you can improve and optimize your results.

THE MONTHLY TRACKER

There are a few key stats that I continually track. I have my own software that calculates the numbers after I input my trades, which is also available to our Minervini Private Access members. My average gain is very important to monitor regularly because I base my risk in large part on that number. I also track my batting average (percentage of profitable trades) (Figure 4-2). If those numbers start to deteriorate, I adjust my stops accordingly. **During a difficult trading environment your gains will be smaller and less frequent than during a healthy market. When this occurs, remember three words (with a nod to Nike): *"Adjust" Do It!*** Always think risk in relation to reward. You must adjust your risk as a function of potential reward.

Monthly Tracker

	AVG GAIN	AVG LOSS	WIN %	TOTAL TRADES	LG GAIN	LG LOSS	AVG DAYS GAINS	AVG DAYS LOSS
JAN	7.78%	3.65%	20.00%	5	7.78%	5.53%	7	10
FEB	17.51%	5.35%	62.50%	8	21.34%	8.15%	24	9
MAR	17.20%	4.91%	55.56%	9	29.87%	7.22%	31	11
APR	9.98%	5.48%	40.00%	10	10.02%	8.23%	13	17
MAY	18.65%	5.50%	54.55%	11	24.79%	13.09%	40	19
JUN	8.32%	4.06%	50.00%	6	12.14%	7.29%	29	11
JUL	16.67%	6.33%	57.14%	14	30.04%	8.04%	44	13
AUG	8.43%	4.26%	33.33%	6	8.77%	7.50%	12	7
SEP	19.61%	6.09%	44.44%	9	26.01%	8.78%	36	12
OCT	-	5.19%	0.00%	4	-	7.47%	-	9
NOV	11.19%	8.00%	50.00%	6	13.43%	11.02%	31	8
DEC	14.21%	6.33%	42.86%	7	18.53%	8.07%	19	8
AVG.				95	18.43%	8.37%	26	11

Trading Summary	
Winning Percentage	46.32%
Average Gain	13.35%
Average Loss	5.85%
Win / Loss Ratio	2.28
Adjusted Win / Loss Ratio	1.97

Figure 4-2 Using a monthly tracker allows me to track my trading results month by month. This helps me keep perspective and troubleshoot my approach day by day.

A Few More Important Numbers to Track

The next relevant numbers are the largest gain and loss in any one month and the number of days my gains and losses are held. I call them the "Stubborn Trader" indicators. Don't pay much attention to any one month, but when you look at the average over a 6- to 12-month period, the net result should be positive. For example, if your largest gainers are smaller than your largest losers on average, this means you're stubbornly holding losses and only taking small profits, the exact opposite of what you should be doing. If your average hold time on your gainers is less than the amount of time you hold your losers, again, it's an indication that you hold onto losses and sell winners too quickly. This is valuable information, but few traders even track these numbers.

Tracking this data will keep you honest and give you a true read on what's happening within your trading. This is the discipline of champion traders. They don't stick their head in the sand; they want to know the truth so they can improve on their weaknesses and optimize their efforts. **By developing emotional distance, separating myself from my results, I gain insight into my trades, without rationalizing or making excuses.** Monitor your results and do the math; as the saying goes: the truth will set you free.

Statistics you should track include

- Average win
- Average loss
- Win/loss ratio
- Batting average (percentage winning trades)
- Adjusted win/loss ratio (adjusted for batting average)
- Largest wins
- Largest losses
- Number of days gains are held
- Number of days losses are held

Your Personal Bell Curve

Over time, it's all about the "curve": the distribution of your gains and losses will determine your performance. Your trading results will distribute along a bell curve, and hopefully your curve is skewed to the right. To maintain a profitable bell curve, your stop-loss should be based on what you have returned on average on your winning trades and how often these wins occur. As I already said, I recommend that you continually track your batting average and average gain and average loss. Doing so will allow you to determine quickly if your recent trading is deviating from your own historical norms and if you're maintaining your losses in line with your gains. This will give you the necessary feedback to make adjustments in response to your losses.

I cannot emphasize enough how valuable this information is in helping you maintain a consistent and profitable long-term trading track record. The more data you have from your trading results, the more significant it is—and the more likely your results will end up close to your assumption over time. Closely tracking your own results allows you to keep a finger on the pulse of your trading.

If I want to contain my losses to 10 percent or less, that means I should see very little to no data to the left of minus 10 percent on my bell curve. On the right side, I want to see as much data as possible. What I'm looking to achieve is a curve "skewed" to the right (Figure 4-3). That means I contain my losses (on the left side of the curve), while I let my profits run (on the right side of the curve). I look at a bell curve of my trades regularly to see if I'm maintaining an edge.

I call the minus-10 percent mark on my bell curve The Wall. Some people call it the Uncle Point. It's the largest loss I ever want to take. Not the average loss, the largest. My goal is to never let losses get through "The Wall." Over time you will have some penetration of your own personal wall. Occasionally, you will have a loss get out of hand due to a fast-breaking stock and slippage. But you should have more data on the right side of your curve than you do on the left side.

Knowledge, as they say, is power. Knowledge of your own trading will empower you, reinforce your emotional discipline, and make you a better trader. It will get you thinking how your gains and losses distribute in relation to each other. As a result, you will make better trading decisions because you will have a vivid picture in your mind of the effect your losses will have on your distribution curve and the toll they take against your gains. Think of your distribution curve as a game of tug-of-war, and you want the "right side" to win the battle.

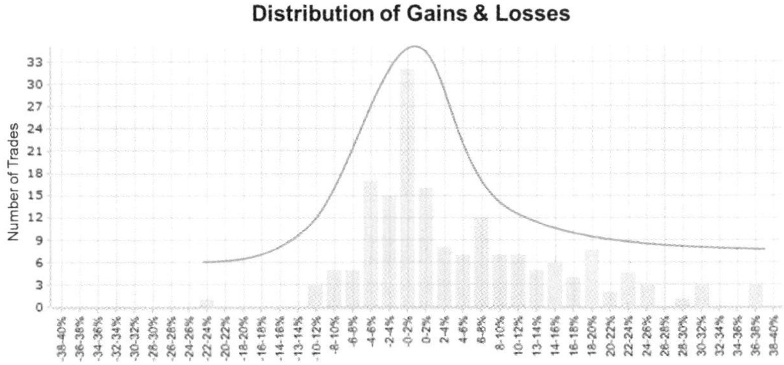

Distribution of Gains & Losses

Figure 4-3   The ideal distribution is to have as many outliers as possible on the right and the fewest on the left, attaining a "skewed" curve.

TURNOVER AND OPPORTUNITY COST

In the stock market, time is money, as is lost opportunity. I learned early that you should not underestimate the power of "small" gains compounded over time. Higher turnover of relatively small gains can mean significantly higher returns compared to lower turnover with higher gains. It's all a matter of what can be accomplished in a given time frame. Let's say within a 120-day period you feel pretty confident that you can find a stock to buy that will go up 40 percent. The question is, can you find three stocks that go up 20 percent or six stocks that go up 10 percent? It's certainly easier to find stocks that go up 10 percent than it is to find a 40-percent gainer. The real question is: does more frequency make mathematical sense? Six 10 percent gains compounded will yield almost double the total return of one 40 percent winner, and just three 20 percent winners will yield almost as much as six 10 percent winners.

The amount of turnover is directly related to the average gains and losses and your batting average. If you're turning your portfolio over very rapidly, you can have smaller gains and losses and a lower win/loss ratio than if you're turning it over less. You're getting the benefit of your "edge" more often. This is the same concept as a retailer who sells a low-priced or low-margin product versus another who sells a higher ticket item with less inventory turnover. The lower-priced merchandise may produce more profit than the higher-priced goods if the retailer can make up for the profit difference through higher sales volume. Day traders work on very small margins, averaging only fractions per trade while making thousands of trades per year, turning over that small edge frequently enough to produce a tidy profit.

As an investor, your merchandise is stocks. Your objective is to buy shares that are in strong demand and sell them at a higher price. How much of a profit margin you make will depend a lot on the type of portfolio you are running. You may be like Walmart, which operates on very small margins but does a tremendous amount of volume. Or you may be like a boutique that offers unique and trendy merchandise and earns higher margins on much lower volume. You may be making numerous trades for a small gain, but by sheer volume you turn in an impressive return at the end of the year. Or you may be a long-term investor with select merchandise that also produces a solid return. **In the end, it all comes down to having your gains on average be larger than your losses, nailing down a profit, and repeating the process. This is the basic objective of any business endeavor.**

Are you looking to bag the big one, even though a handful of smaller profits would make you just as much or even more money? Every strategy is different, so it's important to calculate opportunity cost and determine what the optimal time frame and turnover rate should be. Again, understanding your numbers is the key. So, start doing some math. Analyze your results and optimize your efforts.

A Win/Win Solution
to Protect Your Psyche

As I've already pointed out, a trader's mindset fluctuates mainly between two emotions, indecisiveness and regret. And a trader's emotional state vacillates between greed and fear—and mostly fear. As we've touched on previously, there is the fear of missing out, which leads traders to chase a stock that's already had a big run-up in price. They try to squeeze every dime out of a trade because they're afraid of selling too soon, fearing that a stock they sell at $20 will become the next Google. Or, a stock that they bought at $45 drops to $40 and then to $35, which leads to regret for not selling at $40—so they hang on, hoping the stock will recover some of its lost ground. Compounding this problem, most traders sell too soon and take small profits because they fear the stock is going to erase their gains, but they hold losses because they fear they might sell the stock and it will then turn around and go up.

The only antidote to combat anxiety and calm fears are rules and realistic goals. With steadfast rules, your decisions will not be emotionally based, but grounded in reality. Remember, trading is not about buying at the absolute low and selling at the all-time high. It's about buying lower than you sell, making profits that are larger than your losses, and doing it over and over again. When you fully grasp this foundational aspect of trading, you will remove a big psychological barrier to successful investing.

One of the most common questions I'm asked is when to take a profit, particularly if the stock has made a decent run. Your specific price target of where to sell should be based on technical rules that are part of your specific strategy (Section 9 addresses selling). There is, however, an overarching rule that applies to all strategies: *Protect your psyche!* Don't let yourself become consumed with regret or shackled with indecisiveness.

Deploy the "sell-half" rule.

Let's say a stock you're holding is up 20 percent—twice your average gain of 10 percent and almost three times your risk of 7 percent. You have a nice profit, but you aren't sure if you should sell. You like the company and think it could go higher. But it has just started to slip back a little bit (let's say it was up 25 percent at one point). Indecisiveness sets in as you debate with yourself about what to do. The solution is easy: sell half your position.

Using this example, if you sell half your position at 20 percent, compared to your average gain of 10 percent, it's very difficult to lose on the trade. Half of your trade is booked at a 20 percent profit. Even if you only break even on the remaining half, you will still make 10 percent (right in line with your average gain), and you'll still be ahead of the game. In fact, you could suffer a 10 percent loss on the remaining position and still be okay with no loss on the trade.

After selling half, you can see where the stock goes with the remaining position. No matter the outcome, you are a winner from a psychological standpoint, without any regrets. **When you sell half, if the stock goes higher you say to yourself, "Thank goodness I kept half." If the stock goes lower, you'll say, "Thank goodness I sold half." Psychologically, it's a win/win either way.**

Neutralizing regret is only possible if you sell half. If you sell 75 percent of the position and keep 25 percent and the stock goes higher, you'll have the regret of, "Oh, I wish I kept more." Conversely if you sell less than half and the stock goes lower, you'll kick yourself saying, "Oh, I wish I'd sold more." Sell half and you equalize the rationale and protect your psyche in both directions.

One word of caution—selling half does *not* work on the downside when you're at a loss. When your stop is hit, you get out! You shouldn't sell half on the downside and gamble with the rest of your position, hoping the stock will turn around. When a position moves against you and hits your defensive sell line, there is no wiggle room—only disciplined, decisive action.

RESULTS-BASED ASSUMPTION FORECAST

Your results tell you a lot: where you should be cutting your losses, whether your position size is too big or too small, whether you are improving or doing worse than you have been historically, and how much you are deviating from your goal. To see these insights, however, you must track your stats.

I calculate and track my results regularly. Not only do I know that my average gains have been "x" and my average losses have been "y," I also see my actual returns over time. Then, based on the numbers I see, I can project what I can expect in the future. If these results match my objective, then my approach is good. If I'm falling short of where I want to be, then I can see what adjustments need to be made. Working with actual results, you can experiment with the numbers and determine what is realistic and what is not.

For example, let's say you have a $200,000 portfolio and your position size is 25 percent (Figure 4-4). Your desired return is 40 percent. Your average gain is 14 percent, and your average loss is 7 percent, with a batting average of 46 percent. Now, based on these results, to achieve that 40 percent goal, you would need to do about 60 trades.

INPUTS

Portfolio Size $	$200,000
Position Size %	25%
Desired % Return	40%
Average % Gain	14%
Average % Loss	7%
% of Winning Trades	46%

RESULTS

Avg $ Gain on Winning Trades	$7,000
# of Winning Trades	28
Avg $ Loss on Losing Trades	$3,500
# of Losing Trades	33
Gain / Loss Ratio	2:1
$ Position Size	$50,000
Expected Net % Return per Trade	2.66
Expected Net $ Return per Trade	$1,300
$ Goal	$80,000
# of Trades Needed to Reach Goal	60
Adjusted Gain / Loss Ratio	1.7:1
Optimal f	19.00%

Figure 4-4 Using Result-Based Assumption Forecast (RBAF), you can pinpoint exactly what it will take to achieve your goal and determine how various adjustments will affect the outcome.

Now you need to ask yourself, with your style of trading, how long will it take to find 60 opportunities to trade? Based on your own history, it may be likely that you could find 80 or 90 trading opportunities per year, or maybe more. If so, you have the opportunity not only to achieve that 40 percent, but maybe even double or triple it.

Or, perhaps you think you should change your position size. If you increase your position size to 50 percent, you'll only have to do 30 trades.

If you decrease it to 12.5 percent, you will need to do 120 trades to accomplish the same return. Based on your own results, you can determine what it will take in terms of position size and number of trades to achieve your desired performance.

If you are a short-term trader, you're going to have a lot more trading opportunities. However, your gains and losses will likely be much smaller than those of a swing trader or longer-term investor. You might be in and out for a 1- or 2-point gain or a half-point loss. However, you'll be doing that repeatedly. If you're a long-term term trader, you will have far fewer opportunities, but your average gain will be larger. The key is to figure out the optimum way to maximize your results.

Obviously, to develop a Results-Based Assumption Forecast (RBAF), you need some data; the more the better. When you're starting out, you will not have many results to analyze. So, the sooner you get started, the sooner you will be armed with valuable data.

The most important reason to study your results is for the insight you will gain into yourself. Just as people have different thresholds for physical pain, the same goes for your emotional thresholds when enduring losses or controlling greed. These emotional triggers are what dominate your trading strategy more than anything. Show me one person who takes every single trade that his or her system identifies. Unless you have a black box operating in your trading room and all you do is print out the P&L at the end of the day, your emotions influence your decisions. Your emotional makeup is the thread that goes through everything you do.

Your results, therefore, are the net of *everything*: your strategy, your execution, your commissions, and your emotions. The numbers you see on your spreadsheet are produced by everything that goes into your trading, including your emotions.

What matters, therefore, is the ultimate number—your results. It doesn't matter if your strategy is capable of capturing 100 percent, but you get out after a 10 percent profit. The only thing that matters is the bottom line of your results. And based on what you've done thus far, you can employ a RBAF to determine where you can potentially go and what it will take to get there.

To Compound or Not to Compound

They say if you torture numbers long enough, they will tell you whatever you want to hear. Before you risk your hard-earned capital, I suggest that you not only torture the numbers, but fully comprehend them. When dealing with risk, there are some interesting things to understand, such as whether to compound or not. I show you this example mainly to illustrate how important it is to understand the math behind your trading, because it's powerful stuff. If you don't believe me, consider the following:

Two traders, Larry and Stuart, each start with $100,000. And they each make 24 trades following the exact same system. They buy and sell at the exact same time and at the exact same prices. Twelve of the 24 trades produce a 50 percent gain each. The other 12 trades produce a 40 percent loss each. The gains and losses alternate from up 50 percent to down 40 percent, back and forth, until 24 trades are complete. Now for the results: One trader makes a profit of 120 percent, bringing his account up to $220,000. The other loses 71.75 percent, or $71,750, leaving his account at a measly $28,250. How is this possible?

Trader Larry decides not to reinvest his return. He simply bets a fixed amount each trade (based on the $100,000 capital) and does not reinvest the profits. Trader Stuart, on the other hand, reinvests his capital, thus compounding his returns. Which is the better strategy, to not reinvest or to reinvest and compound? The results might surprise you (see Figure 4-5).

Do What Most Traders Don't Do

A healthier lifestyle, we've all been told, comes from developing healthier habits. It's not the crash diet or suddenly deciding you're going to go out and run a marathon without training. Being healthy is the sum total of all the things you do every day: how you eat, how often you exercise, drinking in moderation, and so forth. In time, you won't even have to make a choice about what to do or not do; your healthy habits will be deeply engrained.

		Non-compounded			Compounded		
TRD	% G/L	$ P/L	CUM BAL	CUM %	$ P/L	CUM BAL	CUM %
			$ 100,000			$ 100,000	
1	50%	$ 50,000	$ 150,000	50%	$ 50,000	$ 150,000	50.00%
2	-40%	$ (40,000)	$ 110,000	10%	$ (60,000)	$ 90,000	-10.00%
3	50%	$ 50,000	$ 160,000	60%	$ 45,000	$ 135,000	35.00%
4	-40%	$ (40,000)	$ 120,000	20%	$ (54,000)	$ 81,000	-19.00%
5	50%	$ 50,000	$ 170,000	70%	$ 40,500	$ 121,500	21.50%
6	-40%	$ (40,000)	$ 130,000	30%	$ (48,600)	$ 72,900	-27.10%
7	50%	$ 50,000	$ 180,000	80%	$ 36,450	$ 109,350	9.35%
8	-40%	$ (40,000)	$ 140,000	40%	$ (43,740)	$ 65,610	-34.39%
9	50%	$ 50,000	$ 190,000	90%	$ 32,805	$ 98,415	-1.59%
10	-40%	$ (40,000)	$ 150,000	50%	$ (39,366)	$ 59,049	-40.95%
11	50%	$ 50,000	$ 200,000	100%	$ 29,525	$ 88,574	-11.43%
12	-40%	$ (40,000)	$ 160,000	60%	$ (35,429)	$ 53,144	-46.86%
13	50%	$ 50,000	$ 210,000	110%	$ 26,572	$ 79,716	-20.28%
14	-40%	$ (40,000)	$ 170,000	70%	$ (31,886)	$ 47,830	-52.17%
15	50%	$ 50,000	$ 220,000	120%	$ 23,915	$ 71,745	-28.26%
16	-40%	$ (40,000)	$ 180,000	80%	$ (28,698)	$ 43,047	-56.95%
17	50%	$ 50,000	$ 230,000	130%	$ 21,524	$ 64,570	-35.43%
18	-40%	$ (40,000)	$ 190,000	90%	$ (25,828)	$ 38,742	-61.26%
19	50%	$ 50,000	$ 240,000	140%	$ 19,371	$ 58,113	-41.89%
20	-40%	$ (40,000)	$ 200,000	100%	$ (23,245)	$ 34,868	-65.13%
21	50%	$ 50,000	$ 250,000	150%	$ 17,434	$ 52,302	-47.70%
22	-40%	$ (40,000)	$ 210,000	110%	$ (20,920)	$ 31,381	-68.62%
23	50%	$ 50,000	$ 260,000	160%	$ 15,690	$ 47,072	-52.93%
24	-40%	$ (40,000)	$ 220,000	120%	$ (18,829)	$ 28,243	-71.76%

Figure 4-5   As this example shows, there are powerful insights to gain from tracking your actual results, knowing the reality of the math behind risk, and not relying solely on assumptions about what you think will happen.

In trading, too, there are healthy routines—I call them Lifestyle Habits—that need to become second nature. Just like getting up in the morning and brushing your teeth or heading to the gym for a workout, these habits will become part of your trading lifestyle. And once developed, these habits will help you progress and expand your comfort zone.

One of the healthy habits of trading is conducting a post-analysis of your results on a regular basis. Another is cutting your losses without fail to protect your capital from devastation. This is more involved than merely keeping a trading log. Regularly analyzing your results provides you with a feedback loop. The basic premise of any feedback loop is that it allows for regulation or self-governing within a system. Feedback also facilitates learning; knowing what has been successful in the past allows you to apply that same approach in the present and future.

For your feedback loop to be relevant, it must be employed consistently and regularly. For example, as part of my post-trade analysis discipline, I do quarterly and annual evaluations to gather as much information about my trades as possible. Your feedback loop must have a schedule, just like your plan. If you only plug in occasionally for feedback, the data will be random and unreliable.

When you're making progress and trading is going well, doing a post-trade analysis is painless; in fact, you'll probably feel pretty good about yourself. But when you aren't trading so well, the analysis gets difficult, to the point that you will probably try to avoid doing it. It's like any other difficult episode, such as working with a psychotherapist to analyze an unsuccessful relationship or a childhood trauma. It's painful! But analyzing what went wrong in that failed relationship or what happened during that difficult phase of your life will yield powerful and even transformative lessons that will help you become more successful in your current life and your future. The same goes for trading; growth comes from having the courage to look at the difficult times and dissect what went wrong.

YOU CAN MAKE MONEY OR YOU CAN MAKE EXCUSES

As you now know, I'm a photographer in my spare time. It's a hobby, but I take my photography pretty seriously, and my goal is to produce great images just as my goal is to produce great results trading. I have state-of-the-art equipment. Not that I think having the best equipment is going to make me a great photographer; it won't any more than a fast car will make someone a great race car driver. But it does eliminate the "excuse factor."

One of the biggest roadblocks to trading success and to success in general can be summed up in a single word: excuses. I want to make sure I take full responsibility for my results in everything I do in life. I know the power of owning my results. So, when I get all the best gear, I have nothing left to do except take responsibility. I can't say that another photographer is producing better pictures than I am because he has a better camera or lens. Taking personal responsibility is the most empowering thing I can do to be a better photographer—and it's the single most important thing you can do to become a super-trader. It's an acknowledgment that you have the ability to respond.

In the stock market, you can make money or you can make excuses, but you can't make both. Do whatever it takes to eliminate your own personal excuses. Your road to success starts by taking responsibility. Don't blame outside factors for your lack of success. The best way to take control of your trading is to understand the math behind your results. This will put you on the road to success, because you will know the truth and become empowered.

COMPOUND MONEY, NOT MISTAKES

You're going to buy things that go to zero and sell things that go to infinity.

—Paul Tudor Jones

When I started trading more than three decades ago, my goal was to make the biggest return in the shortest period of time so I could achieve superperformance. To do that, I needed to learn how to really compound my money. But early on, I committed the typical rookie error: I compounded mistakes instead of compounding capital.

I did what many investors do, committing the deadliest mistake of all: when a stock I held declined in price, instead of cutting my loss, I bought even more. The rationale was that by "averaging down," I could lower my cost, so that when it eventually came back (I assumed it had to come back) I would recoup my red ink even faster than I lost it in the first place. This thinking is common in investing: If you liked the stock at $20 a share, you'll love it at $15. But that's precisely how accounts get blown up and investors go broke, because you're compounding a mistake instead of compounding money.

When a position moves against you and you're at a loss, especially right after you buy, it's simple—you made a mistake. It may be that you're missing an element in your selection criteria, or your timing could be off. Perhaps the general market is under distribution. When you buy more under these conditions, your attempt to "average down" on a losing position is truly "throwing good money after bad," as they say. Unfortunately, it happens all the time. And it wipes out more accounts than just about any other practice in trading.

Many investors know they should cut their losses to control their risk. Yet they convince themselves that they should hang in there: *But it's a bull market! But every time I cut my loss, the stock turns around and goes higher. But, if instead of selling, I buy even more, then I can really make a lot of money when the stock goes up again.* Once again, the fear is of selling and then having the stock turn back up, and thus missing a bigger winner. They equate selling in these circumstances to "chickening out." When this happens, ego is taking over. You want to be right, and you want to believe that you will eventually be right. So you convince yourself it's okay to break the rules. You think to yourself four very dangerous words, "Just this one time."

Welcome to the slippery slope. When you tell yourself, *I'm going to break my rule just this once,* you open the door to losing discipline, because it's never just "one time." It's like an alcoholic saying "just one drink" or an addict saying "just one shot of heroin." Occasionally, this will work, but it's unfortunate, because being rewarded for bad habits only reinforces them. A stock you hold falls by 5, 10, then 20 percent, but instead of obeying your stop-loss, you convince yourself to hold, or worse, buy more. The stock turns around, recovers the lost ground, and goes up 20 percent. You tell yourself you're a trading genius! Oh sure, you took a 20 percent risk—assuming you were even going to sell around that level—for a 20 percent gain. If these are the kind of trades you're making, then I'm afraid you're in for a very rude awakening.

The danger is your stock could be headed for real trouble, then your loss compounds to 30, 40, 50 percent—or more. Chances are, if you did this with one stock, you probably have done it with others as well. In the stock market, when bad habits get rewarded it leads to ruin. If "just this one time" works out, then heaven help you, because you'll convince yourself that the end justifies the means, and you should do it again. Then my friend, you are doomed.

Not All Outcomes Are Created Equal

Here's the easiest and quickest way I know to illustrate this point: Two people attempt to cross a road; one looks very carefully both ways, runs across, and gets hit by a car. The other person covers his eyes and blindly runs right into heavy traffic, but makes it to the other side safely. Does that mean the person who made it safely across the road did a smart thing? What would happen if this scenario was repeated 100 times? Who do you think would have a higher success rate of making it to the other side? The result does not justify the means.

How many times have *you* had a "just this one time" moment? You know what I'm talking about: You're in a losing trade, it reaches your stop, you know you should sell, but you really like the company and you're sure the stock will turn around. So, "just this one time," you tell yourself, you're going to hold a little longer and stretch the rules, even though you know you should just get out. So, you keep holding. Now ask yourself: Have you become rich from these "just this one time" moments?

"Just this one time" violates your rules and undermines your discipline. It's like starting a diet, but after three days you decide to cheat "just this one time," and order dessert at lunch. Pretty soon you've packed away extra calories, and the scale moves in the wrong direction the next morning. Trading is challenging enough without sabotaging your own rules. Staying disciplined means you have to take lots of small losses to protect yourself, which makes you feel like you're going in the wrong direction when you really want to catch a big wave. But "just this one time" will put you on a slippery slope that won't end with one trade, one time. You will eventually get rewarded for breaking a rule, and then you'll bend and break more rules, until you end up like the guy who runs across the highway with his eyes closed and his ears covered—a hood ornament!

You're not going to make just one trade, so don't think in a vacuum. Think about the big picture. **My performance went from mediocre to stellar when I made up my mind and decided once and for all to never have a "just this one time" moment ever again.** I said to myself: That's it, no more, I've had enough! No more breaking rules; it doesn't pay.

STRONG WORDS TO LIVE BY

Paul Tudor Jones is arguably one of the greatest money managers of all time. I have the greatest respect for him. Many years ago, I came across a photograph of him with a sign over his trading desk: "Losers average losers." Those three words contain hugely impactful wisdom: only losers average down on losing positions.

That message struck me for a couple of reasons. First, it's a big statement that you'll be a loser if you average down. But if Paul Tudor Jones makes that statement, then it's probably worth paying attention. Second, if one of the greatest traders of all time needed to post a sign with those words in big letters on his wall, that's evidence of just how seductive it is to "average down," and how important it is to remind yourself not to do it. You know the temptation: a stock you liked at $25 is now $20, so your instinct is to love it all the more—what a bargain! Such thinking, though, is only a delusion to keep from admitting that the stock is going in the wrong direction. Get over your ego—and get out while your loss is small, before it turns into a serious loss. It's true, only losers average losers, plain and simple.

THE 50/80 RULE

To compound money, and not your losses, you need to be aware of an insidious probability I call the 50/80 rule. Here it is: **Once a secular market leader puts in a major top, there's a *50 percent chance* that it will *decline by 80 percent*—and an *80 percent chance it will decline by 50 percent.***

Think about these probabilities for a moment. After a stock makes a huge upward move, it will almost assuredly drop by 50 percent when it ultimately tops out. And it's a flip of a coin whether that downward move will be as much as 80 percent. Once big market leaders top, they experience an average decline of more than 70 percent! I'm not making a point about timing here. This story is a cautionary tale about paying attention to the first loss to hit your radar.

Every major decline starts as a minor pullback. If you have the discipline to heed sound trading rules, you will limit your losses while they're small and you will not throw good money after bad. But if you rationalize all the reasons why your stop should be ignored or why you shouldn't use a stop in the first place, then the damage will be far greater when the stock keeps dropping. And if you "average down" through that drop, thinking, *this stock just has to turn around at some point*, then the uncontrolled losses will devastate you psychologically and eventually decimate your trading account.

Holding onto a sharply falling stock or, worse, buying more when the price goes lower may make you money once, twice, or a few times. But at some point, your stocks will keep on falling (Figure 5-1). You won't have just a loss on your original position; you'll also lose on the additional shares you've bought. At this point, you might really compound your mistakes by convincing yourself, *this has to be the bottom*, so you buy even more! Some investors are so egotistical about accepting mistakes that they double down several times. Amateur traders strive to be right; pros strive to make money.

Figure 5-1   Lumber Liquidators (LL) 2008–2016. The stock was a leader that succumbed to the 50/80 rule, topping out in late 2013 before plummeting more than 90 percent.

The guy who doubles down on a falling stock is the same as the poker player who takes a raise to play a pair of deuces. Holding firm with 2-2 in the hopes of beating another player who is betting strong is a rank amateur move. **Pros play the percentages; they're consistent, and they avoid the big errors. Most of all, they avoid risking money on low probability plays.** They bet when the odds are in their favor and fold when they're not. They're not Monday morning quarterbacks who, after the hand is dead, ask the dealer to see the next card so they can find out if they would have come out a winner if they had held. Pros focus on being consistent. They know that the probabilities will distribute correctly over time, and if they play low percentage hands, they will surely lose.

Buying broken leaders may work for you at some point. But the reality is, you're compounding mistakes—not money—and eventually, this behavior will bite you hard and ultimately destroy any chances you have for stellar performance. That's a guarantee!

THE "CHEAP TRAP"

On a visit to your favorite department store, something catches your eye—a sweater, a jacket, a pair of shoes. The quality is superb, the fit is perfect, and it has a designer label. Then you look at the price tag—ouch! Way beyond your budget. But you know from experience that this store has great sales, so you just wait. Sure enough, a few weeks later, the store advertises a big sale and you receive a loyal customer discount of an extra 20 percent off. On the first day of the sale, you find that item you liked so much—only this time it's discounted by 30, 40, or even 50 percent. You're a happy buyer, at a far lower price.

What works in the department store, however, does *not* apply to the stock market. **When you invest in stocks, something that is suddenly "cheaper" is not necessarily a bargain—but it could trap you in the stock if you're buying solely because it's cheap.** Instead of being a real "find" (like that Armani jacket on sale), a "cheap" stock could be declining for a good reason. If you buy that stock, believing that you've found a great bargain—particularly if you've fallen in love with the company and its story—you're likely to face big losses if the stock keeps dropping. **When you buy a stock because it's cheap, it's difficult to sell if it moves against you because then it's even cheaper, which is the reason you bought it in the first place. The cheaper it gets, the more attractive it becomes based on the "it's cheap" rationale.**

The problem can be one of perception. It's hard to resist the allure of a "cheap" stock, particularly when it's a big name or had been a highflier in the past. You tell yourself, "No way is *that* high-quality company (General Electric, Coca-Cola, Starbucks, etc.) going out of business." But a company doesn't have to go out of business for it to suffer a major decline in its stock price (Figure 5-2). It can go down and stay down—and your position is "under water" for years, and in some cases for decades.

Figure 5-2   Cisco Systems (CSCO) 1990–2016. After topping in 2000, the stock declined by a whopping 90 percent, and then moved sideways for 16 years.

In more than 33 years of trading, I can't tell you how many stocks I've seen plummet and never come back again. Even professional value players struggle with picking lows. Some of the best value managers suffered huge losses in 2008, buying "cheap" stocks on the way down; except those stocks kept falling and got even cheaper. There's no way of telling if a stock is really at the bottom based solely on valuation.

When a stock market leader tops, the stock may look cheap after a period of decline, but it's actually expensive (Figure 5-3). The reason is that stocks discount the future. In most cases, falling stocks that appear cheap turn out to be very expensive, even after the price declines precipitously. Usually the price-to-earnings (P/E) ratio soars *after* the stock suffers a big decline because negative earnings comparisons, or even worse, losses start showing up on the balance sheet. By that time, it's too late.

Figure 5-3   Lumber Liquidators (LL) 2011–2016. When Lumber Liquidators looked pricey the stock tripled, and when it appeared "cheap" it fell 90 percent.

MAKING SENSE OF A SWIFT DECLINE

I've seen it happen countless times: A company seems to have a great story. It's entering new markets, a promising line of new products is being launched, improving margins outpace the competition—all of it adds up to a compelling growth narrative. When the quarterly earnings report comes out, everything looks even better because revenues and profits are up big compared to the prior quarter and the year-ago period.

But the stock immediately *declines*. In fact, it drops significantly. It just doesn't make sense to you. The company is growing and the numbers were great. And, a big well-respected brokerage firm just put the stock on its buy list.

At this point, you may be tempted to believe that the market is wrong, and that you have found a bona fide investment opportunity. You tell yourself that this stock is cheaper than it's been in months, and you should really load up on shares. Why not?

The answer comes down to "differential disclosure," which in this context means you don't know what the big institutional players know (the players responsible for that big drop). In the absence of that knowledge, you'd be wise to stay away.

The term "differential disclosure" is used in forensic accounting. In essence, it means the information reported in one document, such as the company's annual report, differs from what is disclosed in, say, its tax return or in other Securities and Exchange Commission (SEC) filings. Needless to say, it's a red flag when a company says one thing to shareholders and another to the SEC!

Here, I apply the concept of differential disclosure in another context. Let's say the earnings for XYZ Corp. just came out. Results beat estimates by a good margin, and yet the stock drops 15 percent on the largest volume seen in years. When that happens, there is *no possible way* I'm going to buy this stock, even if it was one of the top names on my watch list.

Clearly, there is some "differential disclosure" going on, between what the company reported and how institutional players view those results. It doesn't matter what I think. The institutions are dumping that stock. I want to be in stocks that the institutions are buying, which will propel those shares significantly higher.

Now, it is certainly in the realm of possibility that this pullback will end up being a missed buying opportunity. However, it is more likely that the company has run into some trouble, and what had been a glowing growth story has dimmed quite a bit. We may only find out later and in hindsight. Trading decisions are made in the now. To trade successfully, you can't be a Monday morning quarterback who calls the plays after the fact, when you know how it all turned out. You must manage your risk in real time. In the moment, you have to ask yourself: **If the company is so great, the story sounds wonderful, and the earnings and sales are strong, then why is the stock going down so much?**

In the stock market, there is no truth without believers. That's why you should never buy the story and never buy the numbers without price confirmation. It's simply unnecessary to do so when there are many companies out there that have all the right criteria lined up. To compound your money, and not your mistakes, your goal is to buy on the way up—not on the way down. Even if your strategy involves buying at a support level or a pullback to the moving average, it's better to wait until the stock starts turning up again than to get in when shares are in a nosedive, because you never know how far a stock will fall (Figure 5-4).

Figure 5-4   Crocs (CROX) 2008. On November 1, 2007, Crocs reported earnings up 144 percent. The stock, however, closed down 36 percent that day on the heaviest volume since its IPO. It also ended the week with the largest weekly decline on the largest volume.

With stock trading, the fundamentals and the story are not as important as how institutional investors (the ones that move stock prices significantly) perceive the numbers and the narrative. **Stories, earnings reports, and valuation do not move stock prices; people do. Without a willing buyer, stocks of even the highest-quality companies are just**

worthless pieces of paper. Learn to trust your eyes, not your ears. If the stock's price action is not confirming the fundamentals, stay away!

MOVE THE BALL ACROSS THE NET

> Every great man never sought to be great; he just followed the vision he had and did what had to be done.
>
> —*100 Great Lives*

Now that we've seen how investors compound losses, how can we realize our true goal of compounding money? First and foremost, this objective is accomplished by sticking to your discipline and applying strict trading rules to your strategy. More important, you need to learn how to do what most investors don't do.

When I was in my early twenties, I loved reading books and listening to tapes on business and negotiating. I remember listening to Roger Dawson, who is the head of the Power Negotiating Institute. To stay focused on what's important during a negotiation, he suggested reflecting on what determines the outcome of a tennis match—the movement of the ball across the net. The player who moves the ball across the net and keeps it in play the longest wins the match.

This is true for negotiating and for trading. You must stay focused on what you're trying to accomplish. **Making money is the result of effectively carrying out a well-thought-out plan. Focusing on the outcome will only distract you from the process—the work you need to do to achieve the desired result.** A baseball player at bat needs to stay focused on the ball in order to make contact. Looking up at the scoreboard will distract him from the critical task at hand.

I went from mediocre to a stellar performer when I told myself: *To heck with worrying about the money and obsessing over the scoreboard. I'm just going to focus on being the best trader I can be and sticking to the rules.* Then the money followed.

SMALL SUCCESS LEADS TO BIG SUCCESS

I long to accomplish a great and noble task, but it is my chief
duty to accomplish small tasks as if they were great and noble.
—*Helen Keller*

Big success in life is the result of a series of small successes all linked
together over time. Stock trading is no different. It's not an on-off business. You don't have to make all-or-nothing decisions. You can move in
increments. I rarely, if ever, jump into the stock market with both feet. I
generally start with a "pilot buy," initiating a relatively small position first.
If it starts to work, I may add to the trade or add a couple more names,
and if I have success on a number of trades, I will then increase my overall portfolio exposure and get more aggressive. This is the way you keep
yourself out of trouble and make big money when you're right.

When first entering the market from a cash position, you should not
increase your trading size and overall exposure until you gain some trac-
tion on your initial commitments. I have a very simple philosophy on
scaling up my trading: **If I'm not profitable when I'm 25 percent or 50
percent invested, why would I move up my exposure to 75 percent or
100 percent invested or use margin?** It's just the opposite: I look to scale
down my exposure if things are not working out as planned, or maybe I'll
hold what I currently own.

By following the right trading rules and progressively scaling back
when things aren't working, you'll be trading your smallest when you're
trading your worst. That's controlling risk! But if you add exposure when
things aren't working, then when you're trading at your worst, you'll be
trading bigger size, which can be disastrous.

This discipline is not just defensive. By following this rule, stepping
up your exposure when trades are working, when you're trading at your
best, you will also be trading your larger positions. That's how you achieve
superperformance. Instead of compounding losses, you'll compound
money, but only if you have the discipline to stick to the rules.

Bottom line: there really is no intelligent reason to increase your
trading size if your positions are showing losses. On the other hand,

when things are working, use the profits to finance risk and build on success.

Here's how: I usually start off with a quarter position (see Figure 5-5). On the heels of each win, I double my position size until I'm trading full-size positions. I scale up on winners and scale back on losers.

Figure 5-5   A typical example of how I scale from smaller to larger positions and use profits to finance my increased risk.

If I keep my risk at 2:1, I can be right just as often as I'm wrong and not get in any trouble. If I can scale up three consecutive winning trades—winning on a quarter, half, and one full position will give me the opportunity to finance three full positions and one half position (see Figure 5-6).

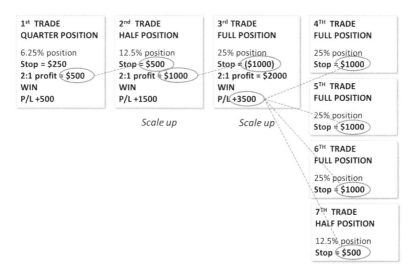

Figure 5-6   By scaling up on the heels of profits, those wins can finance risk on my larger trades.

NEVER LAY ODDS

When you play poker, you should always look at how much is in the pot in relation to how much you are going to bet or call. Good poker players always try to get odds on their money. Would you risk 150 to win 50? Not if you're smart. You would much rather risk $150 to win $550. If your hand has a 50/50 chance of winning, then you need to get better than 2:1 odds on your wager to justify making the bet. Stock trading is no different.

Assuming your trade has a 50/50 chance of success, taking a 20 percent risk to make 20 percent is only going to lead to losses over time; you will break even on the trade, but lose on trading costs. The key is to always get odds, and never lay odds. Keep your risk to a fraction of your gains and you will enjoy a mathematical advantage and have an "edge" (Figure 5-7).

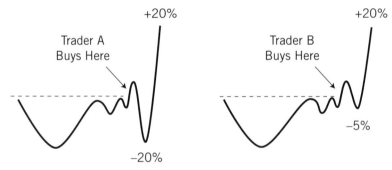

Figure 5-7   Trader A allows the stock to drop 20 percent and then nails down a 20 percent profit, a 1:1 reward/risk ratio. Trader B, in contrast, makes 4:1 on his money, risking 5 percent for a 20 percent return. Which trader do you think will be the bigger winner over many trades?

LONGEVITY IS THE KEY

In my first book, I told the story of achieving a 259 score during my very first year playing in a Wednesday night bowling league. My point was that anyone can have short-term success like I did that night, but I never came close to that score ever again. Consistency differentiates the pros from the amateurs. You may be able to step on the basketball court and hit a three-point shot, but Michael Jordan did it consistently and reliably, and under pressure. Your goal in trading is to execute a strategy you can rely on consistently, knowing that the outcome of any one trade does not determine your success; rather, it's the collective outcome of all your decisions and trades over time. A consistent application of discipline leads to longevity and repeatability.

NEVER LET A GOOD-SIZE GAIN TURN INTO A LOSS

Once a stock moves up a decent amount from my purchase price, I go into profit-protection mode. At the very least, I protect my breakeven point. The rule is never let a good-size gain turn into a loss. Suppose I buy a stock at $50 and the stock advances to $65; I will then move my stop to at least $50. If the stock continues to rise, I start to look for an opportunity to sell all or a portion on the way up to nail down a profit. If I get stopped out at breakeven, I still have my capital; nothing gained, but nothing lost. My priorities in order of importance are:

1. Protect myself from a large loss with an initial stop
2. Protect my principal once the stock moves up
3. Protect my profit once I'm at a decent gain

I have some general guidelines: Any stock that rises to a multiple of my stop-loss and above my average gain should never be allowed to go into the loss column. When the price of a stock I own rises by three times my risk, I almost always move my stop up, especially if that number is above my historical average gain. If a stock rises to twice my average gain, I always move my stop up to at least breakeven, and in most cases I back stop the position equal to my average gain. This will help guard you against losses and protect your profits and your confidence.

It doesn't feel great breaking even on a trade that was once a profit, but it feels a lot better than when you let a good-size gain turn into a losing trade. One of the most demoralizing experiences is to watch a stock you own skyrocket and then tumble, taking back all your profit and then turning into a loss. Remember, your goal is to make a decent profit, not to get in at the low or get out at the high. You need to give your stock room to fluctuate, but you must move your stop up and protect your principal once you have a good-sized gain.

To achieve consistent profitability, you must protect your gains and your principal; I don't differentiate between the two. Once I make a profit, that money belongs to me. Yesterday's profit is part of today's principal.

Amateur investors treat their gains like the market's money instead of their money, and in due time the market takes it back. I avoid this by protecting my breakeven point and my profits when the stock is up a decent amount. Sometimes I nail down a portion of my profits and then free roll the rest for a larger gain. I allow my stock positions enough room to go through a natural reaction, but I never want to hold a stock that is not acting right. But, as I've said, I'm certainly not going to let a good gain turn into a loss (Figure 5-8), and I'm never going to buy more of a stock that has completely wiped out a good-size gain.

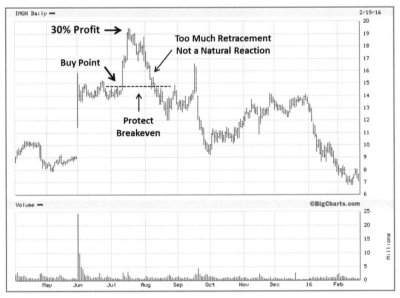

Figure 5-8   Immunogen (IMGN) 2015. The stock fully retraced a 30 percent profit. In this scenario, if you made the mistake of not selling and nailing down a profit when you had the chance—your priority should shift to protecting your principal.

AVOID THE AUDIBLE

The football team is on the 40-yard line. As the offensive linemen take their positions, the quarterback notices a shift in the defense. He suddenly changes his mind about running the play. Just before the snap, he yells out signals to the offense. A new play is instantly put in motion. The ball is snapped, the offensive makes its move, and the team gains 12 yards for a first down.

With the right players and an experienced quarterback, that last-minute change of play, known as "calling an audible," may work well in football. But it is definitely not something you want to do when trading stocks, especially if you are a beginner. Even pros should stick with a plan, with very few exceptions.

An audible, in the case of trading, is rarely a strategic or defensive move caused by a sudden shift in the marketplace. Rather, it means that a trader is making an on-the-spot decision; when money, ego, and emotions are involved, that's rarely a good move. How many times have you made a hasty snap decision that yielded great results?

Even though I've traded professionally for the better part of my adult life—33 years and counting—I never stray from the basics of rule number one of always going in with a plan. I do my homework beforehand. I find stocks that meet the criteria of my strategy. I define my entry points. I know where I'm getting out if I'm wrong, and I know what I need to see to hold. It's a full plan, ready to be executed. That's why my success has been consistent over the years.

This level of preparation cannot compare with a knee-jerk reaction to buy some stock, just because I heard an interview with a company CEO on CNBC or there was sudden breaking news. When I buy a stock, I want to be unemotional, with no pressure to do something quickly or irrationally without thinking it through. When my money is on the line, I'm as fully prepared as I can be to enter the market. **I know from experience that "calling an audible" and making on-the-spot snap decisions can get me into a lot of trouble, simply because I haven't done the full research. So, I don't do it!**

Even when a company appears to have very positive "surprise" news, you never know how the market is going to react. Maybe that news was already priced in. Or maybe the market was expecting something else. When news breaks, volatility rises; wide swings can whip you in and out of a trade. You're likely to get emotional, which doesn't mix well with trading.

Concentrate on executing your plan. If you start tweaking it in the middle of the trading day, you'll be at risk of rationalizing why you should deviate from your original blueprint. That could invite trouble. When you're out of the trade, your head is clear and your emotions are calm— then you can do a thorough analysis of what happened. Based on those insights, you can make improvements to your existing plan and formulate a new plan if necessary. As for calling audibles, they're best avoided.

SHOULD YOU HOLD INTO AN EARNINGS REPORT?

One of the benefits of day trading is going flat at the end of every day and taking no overnight risk. When you swing trade, holding for longer than just an intraday move, you take the risk of news coming out somewhere between when the stock closes and when it reopens the following day. When an earnings report is about to be announced, you open yourself up to the risk of a gap in price. A great report can send a stock soaring, just as a poor report can cause a stock to unravel and decline well below your stop before you can get a chance to react. Why companies are allowed to report earnings after hours, as opposed to during the day when the market is open, is beyond my logical reasoning. But those are the current rules.

My general rule of thumb is never hold a large position going into a major report unless I have a reasonable profit cushion. If I have a 10 percent profit on a stock, then I could usually justify holding into most earnings reports. However, if I have no profit, or worse I'm at a loss, I usually sell the stock or cut down my position size to guard against the possibility of a 10 to 15 percent gap against me. **Regardless of how well you know the company, holding into earnings is always a crapshoot.** I've seen stocks beat earnings estimates by a healthy amount and still get slammed on the open. Bottom line: there's a degree of luck involved when you hold into earnings. If you have a decent profit in the stock, you are at least insulating your principal and mitigating some of the risk. Size positions accordingly and never take big risks going into a major report.

MARCH TO YOUR OWN DRUMMER

The great American writer-philosopher Henry David Thoreau surely was not speaking about trading when he wrote his classic *Walden*. And yet, because Thoreau's wisdom is universal, we can find a direct application to stock investing in one of his most famous quotations: "If a man does not keep pace with his companions, perhaps it is because he hears a different drummer. Let him step to the music which he hears, however measured or far away."

In other words, "March to your own drummer."

All too often traders get pushed into deviating from their strategy and, therefore, making the wrong decisions about their trades because they've succumbed to the influence of outside forces. The marketplace is full of propaganda and hyperbole. Watching television, reading trading commentary, searching the Internet, and keeping up with the latest market letters will inundate you with "news" about what other people are saying.

What some fund manager is doing, or how many trades a friend of yours has made is irrelevant when it comes to your own trading. Your friend might be doing great, making money while you're still waiting for a stock to set up according to your plan. That doesn't mean you should second-guess your approach and do something prematurely just because you're feeling impatient. It doesn't matter what anyone else is doing in the market; the stocks you're watching and trading don't know it.

There are many distractions that can cloud your judgment when trading. Your job is to keep your thinking pure and focused on what matters within your own circle of competence. The hallmark of a pro is to operate within this circle and ignore everything else.

To trade successfully, you must learn to make your own decisions. You need to shut out all the distractions in the market, starting with the talking heads and so-called experts who spend more time "discussing" the market than actually trading it. Your best and most potent immunity is to have a strategy and rules that dictate your actions, so you won't be tempted to follow tips and commentary about a particular stock (Figure 5-9). Can you be assured that the same person who said to buy will be there to tell you when to sell?

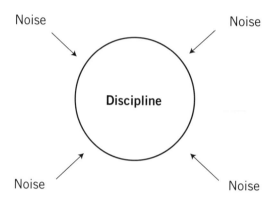

Figure 5-9   Fighting off the penetrating forces that challenge your discipline is even more important than your strategy. Without discipline, you have no strategy, leaving only hope and luck.

Marching to your own drummer means insulating yourself from extraneous influences that would otherwise cause you to deviate from your own discipline. In the words of the late Dr. Wayne Dyer, "be independent of the good opinion of others." If you don't stick with your own rhythm, you'll soon find yourself out of step with your strategy and led astray.

One of the biggest distractors of all is the market itself. You can drive yourself crazy watching the Dow Jones Industrial Average, the S&P 500, Nasdaq 100, and all the rest of the indexes. Just because the index numbers are green and the arrows are pointing up doesn't mean that the stocks you trade are in a buyable position based on your own rules and strategy.

There have been weeks and even months when the Dow was up and yet I did *nothing*, because the stocks on my watch list had not set up according to my strategy. Other times, the Dow was sideways or even down, after digesting a previous big upward move, and I made some of my biggest gains. What the Dow does or doesn't do is little more than background noise. It's certainly not my "drumbeat."

DON'T "FORCE" TRADES

You have your watch list containing the best possible candidates for your next potential trades. Let's say that one or two appear to be setting up nicely according to your criteria. They're almost there—but not quite. So, should you just jump in anyway, because you're impatient, and you figure that it's "close enough" to act? No way! One of my major rules is *never force trades.*

Instead, let the market come to you. Wait for the stock to meet the criteria that your strategy demands. You need patience to confirm that the stock will, indeed, reach the entry point you have identified and behave in the manner that your strategy prescribes. Many times, I've seen a stock almost hit my entry, then reverse course. Had I forced that trade prematurely, I would have been stopped out almost instantly with a loss that was completely unnecessary—and all because I couldn't wait.

If you find it difficult to be on the sidelines, waiting for your setup, remember it's not about the action. *It's about the money.* The problem is, your own need to do something can be the biggest enticement of all to deviate from your plan. You tell yourself, *I'll take a small position.* This kind of self-talk is self-delusion that leads to the very bad habit of "going rogue" instead of sticking to your strategy.

DEVELOP SIT-OUT POWER

Like a cheetah waiting in the bush for the right set of circumstances (a wounded antelope upwind) to pounce on, you must develop what I call sit-out power. This is another hallmark of a pro—the ability to wait patiently for the right set of circumstances before entering a trade. The cheetah can be starving, but it still knows that to eat, it must exercise patience and wait for the right moment. The cheetah is smart enough to know not to waste its energy on a low-probability kill.

If you circumvent your rules and discipline, you have no strategy. If you force trades and, as a result, take losses, you will dig yourself into a hole that will require a lot of work just to climb back to even. Trust your discipline and develop sit-out power. Then, when the moment is right, you make your move. **To make money consistently, you must stay disciplined. Follow your strategy and the trading rules that keep you from entering premature, ill-timed, and risky trades for no other reason than you just want to be in the market.**

LUCK IS FOR VEGAS

If you want to roll the dice, go to Las Vegas. There you will need all the luck you can get. If you want to be successful in the market, you need to remove the "luck factor" as much as possible. How? Once again—do your research. Know what you need to know about the stocks you're buying and be prepared for every outcome before you even enter a trade.

If you love action and you're only interested in "taking a shot," you might get "lucky" in the market. You could even stumble into something at a fortuitous time and make a decent return—without really knowing what you did, how, or why. But how long do you think that kind of luck will last? You can't count on any consistency because there is no real basis to your approach.

The bigger problem with a lucky shot is that it reinforces bad habits. You tell yourself, *this is easy.* You take bigger risks, buying stocks for no other reason than having a "hunch" or because of "something" you heard. It might even work on occasion. Unfortunately, at some point, everybody gets rewarded for a bad habit in the market. In that moment, you feel like you just can't lose. That's the seductiveness of the market: it's like the Venus fly trap that looks so beautiful and then—gulp—it swallows you whole if you fly by the seat of your pants.

Rules trump luck over time. It doesn't matter how much you win on a lucky shot; that end does not justify the means. If you throw a dart at a list of stocks pinned to a dartboard, and you make 30 or 40 percent on the one you "picked," that doesn't mean you made a good decision. You will certainly give back your lucky profits eventually, and your easy money will only be a distant memory. Instead, you want rewards that come from a consistent and sustainable approach that will produce results now and in the future; a strategy that can pay you for life. Luck is a short-term phenomenon. In the long run, luck is for losers.

WINNERS ARE PREPARED

Your fifth-grade teacher was right: do your homework. Every night, I prepare for the next day's trading. That means looking at what I currently own: How are my stocks performing compared to my plan? What new candidates have I identified, and are they nearing the entry point for executing a trade?

If you don't stay on top of your portfolio, you will expose yourself to untold risks: stocks that suddenly gap down on bad news or stocks that are going nowhere, no matter how much the talking heads on television discuss or hype their prospects. I'd rather miss some decent candidates that aren't on my radar or bypass the opportunities that materialize intraday than go in without full preparation and a plan. I need to know all the facts I can before I commit my hard-earned money and take on the risk.

On the flip side, doing my homework thoroughly before the market opens helps me avoid missing those great opportunities. My research casts a net across the market and sifts through the thousands of candidates that meet my disciplined criteria. If the stock doesn't meet my standards, I pass.

When you look at poor performance versus good performance—whether between two individuals with identical approaches, or one individual during two distinct time frames—the differentiating factors are always discipline and consistency. This is as true in trading as it is in professional sports, playing a musical instrument, or starting a company. These same variables always distinguish the great performer from the mediocre one.

The good performer adheres to discipline and consistency, the way a drill sergeant in the army trains the recruits following "standard operating procedure." This discipline and consistency is one of the reasons that the United States has the greatest fighting force in the world. There is no deviation from the routine, no "just this one time" inconsistency in training, performance, or expectation. An army private doesn't get up one day and say, "Sarge, I'm a bit tired today, I think I'm going to pass on our run this morning." There are rules—period. These rules are part of a proven formula for success, which are not circumvented or broken. It's up to you to become your own drill sergeant and keep private first class stock trader true to his or her daily routine. If you want consistent success, you must apply discipline consistently. You can't have one without the other.

HOW AND WHEN TO BUY STOCKS—PART 1

Since 2010, I have had the pleasure of conducting workshops for stock investors interested in learning about my SEPA® methodology. During my lectures, many of the traders often ask my opinion about stocks that are in *long-term downtrends*! I don't need to know anything more about the stock—because I'm not looking to go bottom-fishing for beaten-down shares; I'm certainly not going to try to fight a strong trend.

My starting point is always to have the "wind at my back." That means I only buy stocks that are in long-term uptrends. Although this may seem obvious—for a stock to make a big move up, by definition it's in an uptrend—it's easy to overlook the "big picture" when you're fixated on a myopic view of what you want to see. The danger is you get consumed with the current chart pattern and fail to put it into context. For example, a stock that moves sideways in a strong *uptrend* could be a potential buy candidate. Conversely, a stock that consolidates but is in a strong *downtrend* could be a shorting opportunity. It's all a matter of perspective.

Foundational to my approach is trading *with* the trend (as the old saying goes, "the trend is your friend"). The analogy I often use is "catching a wave," like a surfer. That means having the tide in your favor because swimming against it would be very difficult. While this may seem basic, you need to get this one right *before* you move on to more specific buying criteria.

WHY I USE CHARTS

As part of my annual checkup at the doctor's every year, I get an EKG to determine the health of my heart. Although my doctor can't tell me for sure whether I'm ever going to have a heart attack, as a trained professional he can use this simple procedure of charting the activity of my heart to provide me with valuable information about whether my heart is acting normally or abnormally. This analogy helps me explain to traders the value of using charts.

In examining a graph of a stock's price and volume, we are looking to see if it is acting normally or giving us reason for concern. Charts provide valuable clues. Price and volume analyses can help determine whether a stock is under accumulation or distribution (being bought or sold in size). It can alert an astute chart reader to extreme danger, and it can also indicate when the odds of a potentially profitable situation are relatively high.

The ultimate principle of any auction marketplace is the law of supply and demand. As you learn how to differentiate constructive from faulty price action, you can use charts as a filter to screen your investment candidates to find the best possible selections and improve your odds of success. As you learn to read charts correctly and identify the proper characteristics for a superperformance candidate, the risks and potential rewards become unambiguous. **The key is not knowing for sure what a stock is going to do next, but knowing what it *should* do. Then it's a matter of determining whether the proverbial train is on schedule or not.** That's essential because you know how something is supposed to perform; when it doesn't, the exit decision becomes much clearer and easier.

STAGE 2 ONLY

In my first book, one of the fundamental building blocks I discussed was "Stage Analysis"—and, in particular, the importance of Stage 2. Like all stocks, superperformance stocks go through stages. There are four distinct stages. The cycle through all four could take several years or even decades. The stage you want to focus on is Stage 2. I avoid going long a stock in any stage except Stage 2. During the other three stages (1, 3 and 4), you are either losing money or losing time.

When a stock is in Stage 2, it increases the odds that big buyers are in there supporting the stock. **Based on studies of the biggest winning stocks going all the way back to late 1800s, more than 95 percent of those stocks made their huge price gains while in a Stage 2 uptrend.** That is fact, not opinion. Wouldn't you rather be in sync with a 95 percent probability of a stock being in a big winner, than in the 5 percent club?

I identify the four stages based on what is happening in the stock's price action:

1.   Stage 1: Neglect phase: consolidation
2.   Stage 2: Advancing phase: accumulation
3.   Stage 3: Topping phase: distribution
4.   Stage 4: Declining phase: capitulation

When trading stocks, I have found it invaluable to know the particular stage a stock is in. Focusing on stocks in Stage 2 will put the proverbial wind at your back and in your sails, propelling you forward to successful trading. Aside from the obvious—a stock must be in an uptrend to make a huge gain—using a predetermined trading criteria gives you a framework or baseline to work from so you have a good idea what to expect under specific conditions. You dictate the agenda and, in turn, understand its boundaries (Figure 6-1).

Figure 6-1   Weight Watchers (WTW) 2006–2016. If you bought shares of Weight Watchers in any other stage than Stage 2, you were either sitting with dead money (losing time) or holding losses (losing capital).

THE TREND TEMPLATE

> You don't have to go to business school; you've only got to remember one thing . . . you always want to be with whatever the predominant trend is.
>
> —*Paul Tudor Jones*

When trading great Paul Tudor Jones was asked for his *most important rule* for trading stocks, he said that a stock must be above its own 200-day moving average, and that he would "get out of anything that falls below the 200-day moving average." While this may appear to be a simple rule, such simplicity reinforces humility. No matter how good you are (or think you are), you must remain humble and understand that the market is the engine; if you want to survive over the long term, you'd better learn how to be a caboose!

My Trend Template outlines the criteria I apply to every stock I'm considering. It's my qualifier, or what I refer to as "non-negotiable criteria." Any stock that fails to make the cut is off my radar. No surprise that the first criteria include the price being above the 200-day moving average and having the 200-day in an uptrend. Going long a stock in a downtrend ignores the bigger "health concern" about the stock and its viability as a trading candidate. It's like the doctor pronouncing a patient in perfect health based on low cholesterol and ignoring a cancer diagnosis. Before you invest, demand that your stock be in a healthy long-term uptrend. The following are the eight criteria a stock must meet to be considered in a confirmed a Stage 2 uptrend (Figure 6-2).

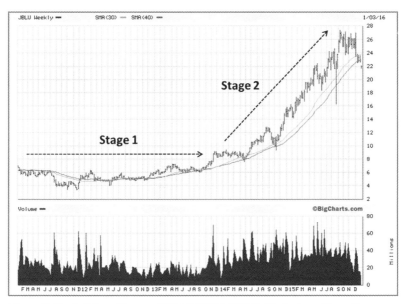

Figure 6-2   JetBlue Airways (JBLU) 2011–2016. While in a Stage 2 uptrend, the stock soared 350 percent.

TREND TEMPLATE CRITERIA

A stock must meet all eight criteria to be deemed in a confirmed Stage 2 uptrend.

1.   Stock price is above both the 150-day (30-week) and the 200-day (40-week) moving average price lines.

2. The 150-day moving average is above the 200-day moving average.

3. The 200-day moving average line is trending up for *at least* 1-month (preferably 4 to 5 months or longer).

4. The 50-day (10-week moving average) is above both the 150-day and the 200-day moving averages.

5. The current stock price is at least 25 percent above its 52-week low. (Many of the best selections will be 100 percent, 300 percent, or more above their 52-week low before they emerge from a healthy consolidation period and mount a large-scale advance).

6. The current stock price is within at least 25 percent of its 52-week high (the closer to a new high the better).

7. The relative strength (RS) ranking (as reported in *Investor's Business Daily*) is no less than 70, but preferably in the 90s, which will generally be the case with the better selections. (Note: The RS line should *not* be in a strong downtrend. I like to see the RS line in an uptrend for at least 6 weeks, preferably 13 weeks or more.)

8. Current price is trading above the 50-day moving average as the stock is coming out of a base.

As the stock transitions from Stage 1 to Stage 2, you should see a meaningful pickup in volume—a sign of institutional support. Looking for stocks that are in verified uptrends allows me to make my first cut and systematically narrow down my potential candidates. Doing this also will help you identify the best stocks with the greatest chances of yielding highly profitable returns. With your hard-earned money on the line, finding superperformance takes a set of criteria based on sound rules and the discipline to adhere to them.

Amateurs, however, very seldom trade this way; when they do, it's rarely consistent. Here's how their thinking goes: They missed the boat on Facebook's big run-up, so now they look for a chance to buy it when it appears to be "cheap." Or they notice Twitter has been going down, so they assume it must bottom sometime soon, because hundreds of millions of people are tweeting all day. People who buy this way are all but guaranteed to do real damage to their portfolios—it's just a matter of time.

Even Pros Can Get It Wrong

With growth stocks, many that appear "expensive" will often get more expensive. "Cheap" stocks, on the other hand, tend to get even cheaper, especially if the stock is in a Stage 4 downtrend. That's why trying to buy at the lowest price rarely turns out to be the best price.

If you are looking for those few gems that have the potential to be real superperformers, you probably are going to have to pay a premium—and that means the stock will likely already be moving up. A stock that is growing at a fast rate and, therefore, likely to gain more ground, will command a higher valuation—just like a Ferrari costs more than a secondhand Hyundai. Don't expect to find those gems in the discount rack. When a stock falls precipitously and drastically underperforms the market, it's usually a warning—not a bargain.

Billionaire investor Bill Ackman learned this lesson the hard way. When Valeant Pharmaceuticals International (VRX) (Figure 6-3), one of his prized investments, turned down sharply and fell below its 200-day

Figure 6-3   Valeant Pharma Intl. (VRX) 2015. By keeping away from this stock when it was trading below its 200-day moving average, you would have avoided a more than 90 percent decline in value.

moving average, Mr. Ackman doubled up. It appears he believed he was smarter than the market or else had fallen in love with the Valeant story to the point of ignoring the danger signals.

From the week in September 2015 when VRX closed below its 200-day moving line, Valeant shares fell a whopping 92 percent. In retrospect, following the simple rule of avoiding stocks below their 200-day moving average would have saved Mr. Ackman and his high net worth investors a fortune. The market has a way of humbling those who think they are so smart they can ignore its verdict. Stick with stocks in Stage 2 uptrends, and you will be much more likely to find an exceptional winner and avoid a bomb like Valeant.

BEWARE THE SERIAL GAPPER

David Ryan, my co-instructor at the 2015 Master Trader Program in Myrtle Beach, South Carolina, and I were discussing the characteristics and dangers of stocks in long-term downtrends. David pointed out to the audience that these stocks often turn into what he calls "serial gappers." These are stocks that move steadily downward and experience a large number of gaps lower along the way. **When you buy a stock in a downtrend, you don't just own a stock headed in the wrong direction. Even worse, you dramatically increase your overnight risk and the chance that you'll wake up one morning to find your stock down big on a gap.**

When stocks show signs of topping and transition into a Stage 4 decline, downside gaps can become the norm. This is the opposite of what you are trying to achieve. As a stock investor, you want to put yourself in a position for happy surprises, not bombs. This starts with avoiding stocks in a downtrend to increase your chances of avoiding the serial gappers.

I shorted KORS at the end of the day, just before the first gap (see Figure 6-4) when it broke below the 200-day line and was about to close right on the low for the day. Being short, this serial gapper turned into a very profitable trade. But imagine what happened to those who were bottom fishing and bought the stock.

Figure 6-4   Michael Kors Hldg. (KORS) 2014. Once the stock price traded below the 200-day line and entered Stage 4, it became a classic "serial gapper." Its share price fell from above $85 to below $35.

If your goal is to own the next superperformance stock, a long-term uptrend is important as your first threshold or qualifier because you're looking to buy stocks that already have some upward momentum. The uptrend test gives you evidence that the large institutions—the players who can really propel a stock higher—are active in the stock. To achieve large returns, your timing must become precise. That kind of precision starts with a stock moving in your direction, so that you can pinpoint a high-probably entry point when the uptrend is likely to be the strongest, which increases your odds of being in the next superperformer.

VOLATILITY CONTRACTION PATTERN

Once I determine a stock is in a confirmed Stage 2 uptrend—it meets all eight of my Trend Template criteria—I look at the current chart pattern. Specifically, I'm looking for a digestion period or consolidation of the previous gains made during the uptrend—or for what I call a volatility contraction pattern (VCP) to develop. I came up with the VCP concept because I saw so many people relying on patterns that seemed to trace the general appearance of a constructive price base, but they missed some of the most important elements of the structure, which can make it invalid and prone to failure.

Throughout my career, I have found that almost every failed base can be traced back to some faulty characteristic that was overlooked. Many books superficially describe technical patterns, and pattern recognition exercises will often lead you astray if you lack an understanding of the supply and demand forces that give rise to high-probability setups.

The most common characteristic shared by constructive price structures (stocks that are under accumulation) is a contraction of volatility accompanied by specific areas in the base where volume recedes noticeably. Determining a correct VCP is the key to establishing the precise point and time to enter a stock. In virtually all the chart patterns I rely on, I'm looking for volatility to contract from left to right. I want to see the stock move from greater volatility on the left side of the price base to lesser volatility on the right side.

During a VCP, you will generally see a sequence of anywhere from two to six price contractions. This progressive reduction in price volatility, which is always accompanied by a reduction in volume at specific points, signifies that the base has been completed. For example, a stock will initially come off by, say, 25 percent from its absolute high to its low. Then the stock rallies a bit, and then sells off 15 percent. At that point buyers come back in, and the price rallies a bit more within the base. Finally, it retreats by 8 percent.

As a rule of thumb, each successive contraction is generally contained to about half (plus or minus a reasonable amount) of the previous pullback or contraction. Volatility, measured from high to low, will be greatest when sellers rush to take profits. As sellers become scarcer, the price correction will not be as dramatic, and volatility will decrease as the price makes its way to the right side of the base. Typically, most VCP setups will be formed by two to four contractions, although sometimes there can be as many as five or six. This action will produce a pattern, which also reveals the symmetry of the contractions being formed. I refer to each of these contractions as a "T."

THE CONTRACTION COUNT

Here's what's happening with successive contractions. Imagine you've soaked a towel in water and then wrung it out. Is it completely dry? No, it's still wet and contains some water. So you retwist the towel to wring it out some more. After more water comes out, is it dry now? Probably it's at least damp. As you keep twisting and wringing the towel to get all the water out, each time the drops will be less and less. Finally, the towel is dry and much lighter.

Similarly, with each contraction in a VCP, the price of the stock gets "tighter"—meaning, it corrects less and less from left to right on successively lower volume as the supply diminishes. Like the wet towel being wrung dry, as a stock goes through several contractions, it becomes lighter and can move in one direction much more easily than when it was weighed down with lots of supply.

Here's how it works in real life: In September 2010, Bitauto Holdings Ltd (BITA) emerged from a well-defined VCP pattern. The consolidation period lasted eight weeks, correcting 28 percent, then 16 percent, and finally just 6 percent on the far right. In Figure 6-5 note the volume contraction during the tightest portions of the setup and on the far right of the base where the price is tightest.

As the stock moves through the $17 area, you can see how fast it advances with little resistance. The reason is that supply has stopped coming to market. With little supply available, even a small amount of demand can move the stock up. And if your long-term work is accurate, and big institutions are indeed in there accumulating the stock, the sky could be the limit. This is a vital concept for successfully timing your buys.

A price consolidation represents a period of equilibrium. As strong investors replace weak traders, supply is absorbed. Once the "weak hands" have been eliminated, the lack of supply allows the stock to move higher because even a small amount of demand will overwhelm the negligible inventory. This is what the legendary trader Jesse Livermore called "the line of least resistance."

Figure 6-5   Bitauto Holdings Ltd (BITA) 2013. A classic VCP pattern that skyrocketed 465 percent in just 10 months.

Tightness in price from absolute highs to lows and tight closes with little change in price from one day to the next and from one week to the next are generally constructive. These tight areas should be accompanied by a significant decrease in trading volume. In some instances, volume dries up at or near the lowest levels established since the beginning of the stock's advance. This is a very positive development, especially if it takes place after a period of correction and consolidation, and is a telltale sign that the amount of stock coming to market has diminished. A stock that is under accumulation will almost always show these characteristics (price tightness with contracting volume). This is what you want to see before you initiate your purchase on the right side of the base, which forms what we call the pivot buy point.

THE TECHNICAL FOOTPRINT

As it goes through a consolidation period, each stock makes its own unique mark. Similar to a fingerprint, these patterns look alike from afar, but when you zoom in and look at the nuances, no two are identical. The resulting signature or silhouette is what I call the stock's technical footprint. The immediate distinguishing features of the VCP will be the number of contractions that are formed throughout the base, their relative depths, and the level of trading volume associated with specific points within the structure. Because I track hundreds of names each week, I created a quick way to capture a visual of a stock by quickly reviewing my nightly notes and each stock's footprint abbreviation.

This quick reference is made up of three components:

1. **Time.** The number of days or weeks that have passed since the base started.
2. **Price.** The depth of the largest correction and narrowness of the smallest contraction at the very right of the price base.
3. **Symmetry.** The number of contractions throughout the entire basing process.

Just as you could get a mental picture of a man simply by being told he was six-foot-five, weighed 284 pounds, and had a 46-inch waist (Figure 6-6), knowing a stock's "measurements" gives you a visual of its footprint. I use this signature to help me understand certain key aspects of the price base, even without looking at the chart.

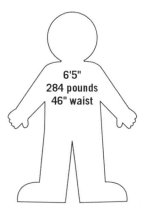

6'5"
284 pounds
46" waist

Figure 6-6   Just as an individual's physical description gives you a mental picture, a stock's "measurements" can give you a visual of the footprint of its price base.

THE VCP FOOTPRINT AT WORK

To illustrate how this technical footprint works, let's look at Netflix (NFLX) just before it made a more than 500 percent move in just 21 months (Figure 6-7). After rallying sharply off the 2008 bear market lows, the stock established a well-defined uptrend—clear evidence that big institutions were accumulating the stock. These big players saw mom-and-pop video rental stores, regional chains, and even Blockbuster Video being challenged by a newcomer called Netflix, which rented movies online—a model that accelerated its sales and earnings dramatically.

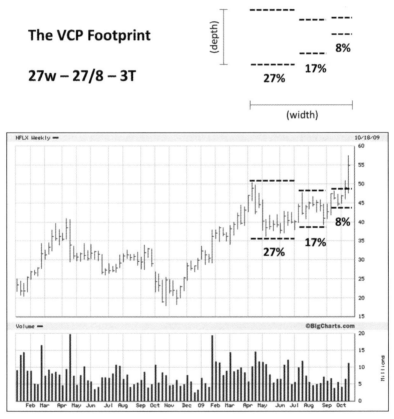

Figure 6-7   Netflix (NFLX) 2009. Netflix's VCP "footprint" reveals a constructive price consolidation. From this point, the stock gained 525 percent in 21 months.

Little did most people know at that early stage, brick-and-mortar video rental was about to become extinct. A paradigm shift was happening in this business, and Netflix had no competition in its new niche because the company invented the category. This meant big potential for sales and earnings, equating to big stock performance.

You didn't have to know everything about the video rental market or be a retail analyst to see the opportunity. Netflix contracted three times (a 3T) before it emerged out of its 27-week (27W) consolidation. In October 2009, I was buying Netflix shares aggressively, even though it was trading at 32x earnings while Blockbuster traded at just 2x earnings. The fact that Netflix looked "expensive" was one reason why most people missed this opportunity just before its best days. Most amateurs and even many pros want to buy the "cheaper" stock. This is based on a complete misunderstanding of how Wall Street actually works. From the time it went public, Netflix soared more than 3,400 percent. During the same period, Blockbuster's stock price lost 99 percent of its value.

Now let's look at Meridian Bioscience (VIVO). In the midst of a Stage 2 uptrend, this stock underwent a series of volatility contractions as it consolidated before continuing its upward run. Meridian Bioscience contracted four times (4T) before it emerged out of its 40-week (40W) consolidation and advanced more than 100 percent over the next 15 months.

Figure 6-8 shows four periods of volatility contraction within the base, which are framed by the dotted lines. The first period started in April 2006, when the stock declined from $19 a share to $13, correcting 31 percent from high to low. The stock then moved higher and consolidated again, falling from just under $17 to below $14 a share for a 17 percent pullback. This is the first sign of contracting volatility. After the second pullback, the stock rallied once again, this time to just above $17 a share, then it pulled back to below $16, a much tighter price range of about 8 percent. At this point, I began getting interested in the stock.

Finally, a short and narrow pullback of just 3 percent over two weeks on very low volume formed the pivot buy point. This told me that selling activity had dried up. Profit-taking had been exhausted as incremental supply coming to market had abated. After putting in 4Ts with successive decreases in volume, the stock price was primed to spike if buyers came in, demanding inventory. In January 2007, I jumped onboard as Meridian Bioscience cracked above the pivot buy point at $17 a share on a noticeable increase in volume; it proceeded to advance 118 percent over the next 15 months (Figure 6-8).

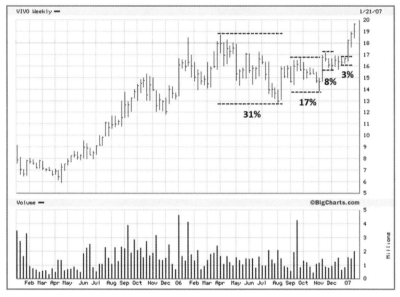

Figure 6-8   Meridian Bioscience (VIVO) 2007. After forming a textbook (4T) VCP pattern, Meridian Bioscience gained 118 percent in 15 months.

OVERHEAD SUPPLY

As a stock corrects and heads lower, inevitably there are "trapped" buyers who bought higher and are now sitting with a loss (Figure 6-9). Trapped buyers agonize over their deepening paper losses and hope for a rally to sell. As their losses grow and more time passes, many of these buyers would be delighted just to get even. This is what creates overhead supply in a stock—investors who want out on a rally or around their breakeven point. They can't wait to sell; after that roller-coaster ordeal, they are thrilled just to get out at breakeven.

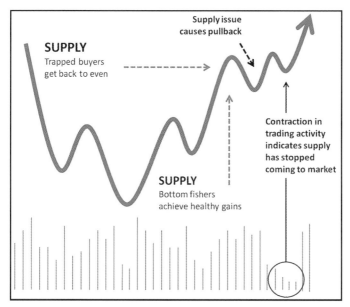

Figure 6-9 Theoretical example of the supply/demand dynamics a stock goes through as it consolidates constructively.

Adding to the supply is another group of buyers who, unlike the trapped buyers sitting at a loss and waiting to break even, were fortunate enough to bottom-fish the stock; now they are accumulating nice short-term profits. As the stock trades back up near its old high, and as the trapped buyers are getting even, the profit-takers also feel the urge to sell and nail down a quick buck. All this selling creates a price pullback on the right side of the base. If the stock is indeed being accumulated by institutions, these contractions will get smaller from left to right as available supply is absorbed by the bigger players' appetites for stock. This is simply the law of supply and demand at work, an indication that the stock is changing hands in an orderly manner.

Before buying, you should wait until the stock goes through a normal process of shares changing hands from weak holders to stronger ones. **As a trader using a stop-loss, you are a weak holder. The key is to be the last weak holder; you want as many of the weak hands as possible to exit the stock before you buy.**

You can tell supply has stopped coming to market by the significant contraction in trading volume and significantly quieter price action as the right side of the base develops. Demanding that your stock meet these criteria before you buy improves the likelihood that your stock is off the public's radar, which helps you avoid a "crowded trade" and increases your chances of success. If the stock's price and volume don't quiet down on the right side of the consolidation, supply most likely is still coming to market, making the trade too risky and prone to failure.

What Does VCP Tell Us?

To recap, the VCP is evidence of the laws of supply and demand at work as the stock goes through an orderly process of changing from weak hands to strong hands. During the volatility contraction, increasingly less supply comes to market. As willing long-term buyers meet eager short-term sellers, the overhead supply that has been holding the stock back dissipates.

It's important to keep in mind that the VCP occurs within the confines of an uptrend. The VCP is going to happen at *higher levels*, after the stock has already moved up 30, 40, 50 percent or even much more, because the VCP is a continuation pattern as part of a much larger upward move. **A stock that is under accumulation will almost always show VCP characteristics. This is what you want to see before you initiate your purchase on the right side of the base, which forms what we call the *pivot buy point*.** Specifically, the point at which you want to buy is when the stock moves above the pivot point on expanding volume.

The Pivot Point

A pivot point is a "call-to-action" price level. I often refer to it as the optimal buy point. A pivot point can occur in connection with a stock breaking into new high territory or below the stock's high. A proper pivot point represents the completion of a stock's consolidation and the cusp of its next advance. In other words, after a base pattern has been formed, the pivot point is where the stock establishes a price level that acts as the trigger to enter that trade. Now, the stock has moved into position for purchase. A temporary pause allows you to set a price trigger to enter your buy. For example, a trader might put in a limit order to buy 1,000 shares if the price breaks the upper range of the pivot point. You want to buy as close to the pivot point as possible without chasing the stock up more than a few percentage points. Then, as the stock trades above the high of the pivot, this often represents the start of the next advancing phase.

When a pivot aligns with the line of least resistance, a stock can move very fast once it crosses this threshold. As a stock breaks through this line, the chances are the greatest that it will move higher in a short time. This often occurs because the pivot point is where supply is low; therefore, even a small amount of demand can move the stock higher. Rarely does a correct pivot point fail coming out of a sound consolidation in a healthy market.

Figure 6-10 shows Mercadolibre (MELI) and its technical footprint of 6W 32/6 3T, meaning that the basing period occurred over six weeks, with corrections that began at 32 percent and concluded at 6 percent at the pivot. As the chart illustrates, in November 2007, the stock underwent a price shakeout and proceeded to tighten up in a constructive fashion. Notice, too, how the last contraction was accompanied with little volume as a dearth of stock changed hands during the last (T) where the pivot point forms. Then, after charging through the pivot point, Mercadolibre's stock price shot up 75 percent in just 13 days. This is the type of rapid price escalation I'm interested in capturing because of the potential to really compound money and achieve superperformance.

Volume at the Pivot

Every correct pivot point develops with a contraction in volume, often to a level well below average. In addition, there will be at least one day when volume contracts very significantly, in many cases to almost nothing or near the lowest volume level in the entire base structure. In fact, we want to see volume on the final contraction that is below the 50-day

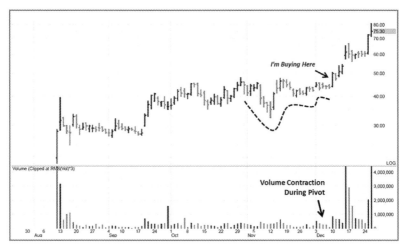

Figure 6-10   Mercadolibre (MELI) 2007. I bought this stock just before it advanced 75 percent in only 13 days.

average, with one or two days when volume is extremely low; in some of the smaller issues, volume will dry up to a trickle. Although often viewed by many investors as a worrisome lack of liquidity, this is precisely what occurs right before a stock is ready to make a big move. As stated previously, when very little supply is available, even a small amount of buying can move the price up very rapidly. That's why you want to see volume contracting significantly during the tightest section of the consolidation (the pivot point).

Consider the example of Michaels Companies Inc. (MIK) (Figure 6-11). The technical footprint of 19W 16/3 4T indicated a 19-week base with successively tighter pullbacks of 16 percent, 8 percent, 6 percent, and then 3 percent. Not only was the last contraction tight in terms of price (a 3 percent fluctuation), but volume was dramatically lower than average. As Figure 6-11 illustrates, this is a very constructive sign. Just as the price broke above the pivot, that's where I placed my buy order.

In the next section, the discussion of how and when to buy stocks continues.

Figure 6-11 The Michaels Companies (MIK) 2014.

.

HOW AND WHEN
TO BUY STOCKS—PART 2

Most constructive setups correct between 10 percent and 35 percent, some as much as 40 percent. Very deep correction patterns, however, are failure prone. You will have more success if you concentrate on stocks that correct the least versus the ones that correct the most. When a stock declines precipitously, the cause is often a serious problem, whether in the company or in its industry; perhaps it's the beginning of a bear market. Just because a stock is trading down 50 to 60 percent off its high, don't give in to the temptation of thinking this is a bargain. First, such a decline could indicate a serious fundamental problem is undermining the share price—a problem that may not be evident in reported or "surface" fundamentals. Second, even if the fundamentals are not yet problematic, a stock that experiences a deep sell-off must contend with a large number of potential sellers or overhead supply. The more a stock drops, the more it is burdened by this overhang.

During major bear market corrections, some stocks can decline by as much as 50 percent and still work. But I rarely buy a stock that is down that much. A stock that has corrected 60 percent or more is off my radar, especially because a decline of that magnitude often signals a serious problem. **Under most conditions, stocks that correct more than two and a half or three times the decline of the general market should be avoided.**

A recent example is GoPro, which makes action cameras (the kind people can strap on their heads while rock climbing). This stock peaked at over $90 a share in October 2014, then sold off sharply to under $40 in March 2015 (Figure 7-1). The big warning in GoPro came when the stock price fell more than 60 percent while the Nasdaq Composite was up 10 percent—a huge underperformance. The issue then became overhead supply. With all those trapped buyers at higher prices, there were a ton of potential sellers. With the stock down so much and drastically underperforming the market, that meant institutions were dumping the stock in anticipation of poor fundamental performance.

From there, GoPro rallied a bit to $65 in August 2015, but compared to where the stock had been, it was still about 30 percent off its peak. Anyone who focused on only the stock's rise might have been tempted to buy the stock. But considering that at $65 it was still nearly a third off its highs in a long-term downtrend, GoPro was not a buy candidate in my book, and I discouraged many of my clients from buying it during this period. As of this writing, GoPro is trading around $9 a share, off more than 90 percent from its peak.

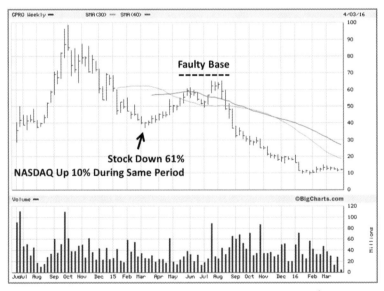

Figure 7-1 GoPro (GPRO) 2015. The stock fell from above $98 a share to under $9. Through the entire decline, the stock was never once in a Stage 2 uptrend.

GoPro is a cautionary tale for traders who fall in love with a stock too easily. Everybody loved GoPro when it topped $90 and looked like it was heading to $100 and beyond. And when it went down, everybody loved it even more, thinking it was only a matter of time before it rose again and returned to its highs—but the rally was a short-lived one. Why? Because GoPro was in a strong downdraft; it did not have the proverbial wind in its sails.

True, GoPro's stock price was above its own 200-day (40-week) moving average, but it did not meet all the Trend Template criteria: the 150-day line was below the 200-day, and both were trending down. Granted, you might pick a stock in a downtrend that turns around and goes into an uptrend. But why take that risk and play guessing games when there are plenty of stocks already in uptrends? Focus on stocks that have already proved themselves, and you will have a much better chance of finding the next superperformer.

BIG WINNERS MUST MAKE NEW HIGHS

One of the most common phrases you'll hear in the stock market is "buy low and sell high." These words have become synonymous with the way most people think about how to make money in stocks. Of course, it's obvious that you must buy at a price lower than the price at which you sell to make a profit. However, this does not mean that you have to buy at or near the lowest price at which a stock has traded historically. Markets are correct far more often than personal opinions or even expert forecasts. A stock making a new 52-week high during the early stages of a fresh bull market could be a stellar performer still in its infancy. In contrast, a stock near its 52-week low at best has overhead supply to work through and lacks upside momentum. But a stock hitting a new high has no overhead supply.

There are those of you who say, "I don't want to wait until the Stage 2 criteria are confirmed." You want to try to get in early, when the stock is moving off its lows. The problem here is that there is no confirmation in the early stages. How do you know that the stock is attracting institutions? Even a good start can get derailed if the fundamentals aren't there. Instead you end up buying a bounce that fizzles, and the stock stays in Stage 1 limbo or, worse, breaks down and declines. In the following example (Figure 7-2), you can see how the real excitement doesn't even start until the stock starts hitting all-time price highs.

Monster Beverage (MNST) registered an all-time high in late 2003. If you were afraid to buy the stock because it appeared too expensive or too "high," you would have missed a huge opportunity: The stock price advanced 8,000 percent by early 2006. **Keep in mind that the only way a stock can become a superperformer—moving from, say, $20 to $80 and then to $180—is for that stock to make a series of new highs all the way up.**

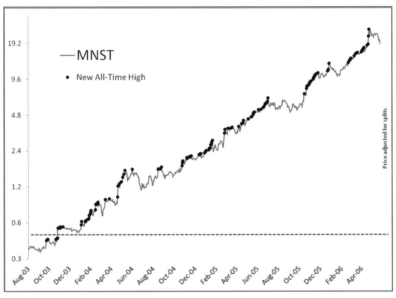

Figure 7-2   Monster Beverage (MNST) 2003–2006. Made an all-time high in August 2003 and then rallied more than 8,000 percent.
Chart courtesy of Longboard Asset Management.

How to Correctly Use Relative Strength

Investor's Business Daily (IBD) has made it very easy to compare the relative strength (RS) of a company to others in the market, with a simple ranking of 1 to 99 (99 being the strongest and 1 the weakest). It's true that you want to concentrate on names with strong RS, but that does not mean that you should focus only on the RS number in IBD. The key is to use a combination of the RS ranking, the RS line (which compares stocks to the general market), and the technical action of the stock itself. These indicators will help you determine the best time to make your purchase—ideally, when a stock is outperforming the general market, while emerging from a sound consolidation with proper VCP characteristics. If you concentrate on the ranking only, you could end up buying stocks that have moved up too fast or too much and are vulnerable to a large pullback or correction.

KNOWING WHAT TO LOOK FOR—CASE STUDIES

People think you need to have a crystal ball or react at a moment's notice to fast-breaking news stories to catch a profitable stock move. Not true. In many cases, the writing is on the wall for weeks, months, and sometimes for years leading up to a well-defined buy point. You just need to know what to look for.

Following are a few case studies of stocks I bought, what I was looking at before I made my purchase, and the important factors that foretold superperformance potential before they made their big moves.

AMAZON.COM

In October 2001, Amazon (AMZN) carved out its low and the stock bottomed. Subsequently the price ran up dramatically, causing the 200-day (40-week) moving average line to turn up. This marked the beginning of a new up leg and, based on my Trend Template, the stock was now in a confirmed Stage 2 uptrend. I began to get interested.

In Figure 7-3, you will notice that from the point that AMZN bottomed, the RS line turned up and maintained a persistent uptrend throughout the first up leg. By May 2002, the stock was up more than 300 percent from the lows in just eight months, which probably led many to conclude the stock was out of buy range. To the contrary, the stock was only in the early stages of a proper setup. The first up move gave the stock the momentum I was looking for, and it was clear institutions were buying heavily.

From May 2002 through October 2002, the stock formed a perfect 3-C (cup completion cheat) pattern. A tip-off that the stock was destined to emerge was the RS line moving into new high ground before the stock started breaking out of its base. Knowing the RS line was in an uptrend since November 2001, I wouldn't even have to see the RS ranking in IBD to know that this stock was at the very top of the list. On October 10, 2002, the stock moved above the pivot buy point, emerging from a 22-week base. That's where I established my position, the exact day the market bottomed after a 31-month bear market. A coincidence, you say?

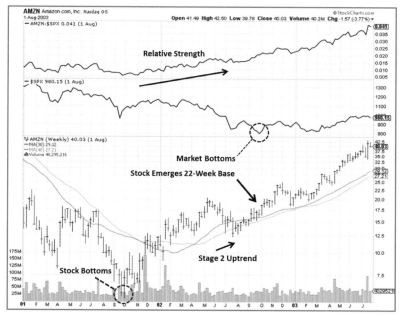

Figure 7-3   Amazon.com (AMZN) 2001–2003. On October 10, 2002—the exact day the market bottomed—Amazon emerged from a 3-C pattern and then rose 1,700 percent in 16 months.

LEADERS BOTTOM FIRST

Market leaders often emerge from consolidations around the time the general market is coming off a bear market or correction low. Sometimes it's a little before the low, and sometimes it's a month or two after. Many times, I've seen a leader emerge right on the first up day after the absolute low in the broad market. Amazon did just that. It then shot up 240 percent in just 12 months and went on to make a 38-fold advance.

The best stocks make their lows *before* the general market averages do. During a correction, as the major market indexes make lower lows, the leaders diverge and make higher lows. The stocks that hold up the best and rally into new high ground off the general market low during the first four to eight weeks of a new bull market are the true market leaders, capable of making spectacular gains.

But there are a few reasons why you could miss the best stocks. In the early stage of new leader's uptrend, there may not be much confirming price strength from other stocks in its industry group. This is normal. Often there will be only one or two other stocks in the group displaying strong RS. **Some of the market's biggest winners are part of broad industry group moves, but often by the time it's obvious that the underlying sector is strong, the real leaders—the very best of the breed—have already moved up dramatically in price.**

As a bear market is bottoming, leading stocks that best resisted the decline will turn up first and break out from their bases. Most investors fail to take notice of this phenomenon and refuse to acknowledge buy points in leading stocks because they're gun-shy after the market's steady declines. Just about the time the market bottoms, most investors have suffered large losses in their portfolios because they refused to cut them short during the previous correction. After a bear market decline, many investors are too busy hoping to break even on the open losses they hold—thoroughly convinced that the end of the world is coming because their investments got crushed due to a lack of sell rules. As a result, they want no part of acknowledging fresh new buy signals and miss a golden opportunity.

Making it even more difficult to recognize a proper buy point is the fact that, once again, leading stocks always appear to most investors to be too high or too expensive. Market leaders are the stocks that emerge first and hit the 52-week-high list just as the market is starting to turn up. Few investors buy stocks near new highs, and fewer buy them at the correct time. They focus on the market instead of the individual market leaders and often end up buying late and owning laggards.

EBAY—2003

Some leaders bottom before the general market and then emerge from a constructive base after the market indexes establish their lows. For example, eBay bottomed in late 2000, well before the market carved out its low in October 2002. Shortly thereafter, eBay consolidated in a relatively tight seven-week base. By this time, the stock was in a confirmed Stage 2 uptrend and sported a top-tier RS ranking. As Figure 7-4 illustrates, the RS line was in a long-term uptrend, moving into new high ground well in advance of the stock price. This was an important tip-off that the stock was likely being accumulated by big institutions. From the point eBay emerged from its seven-week base, the stock price advanced 234 percent in just 24 months.

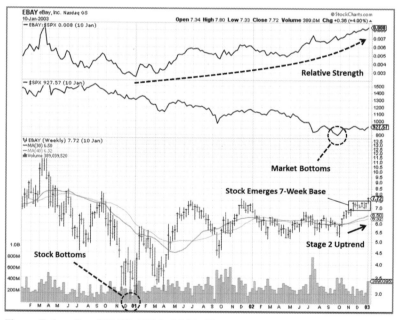

Figure 7-4   eBay (EBAY) 2000–2002. The stock bottomed in 2001 and didn't form a reliable base until late 2002. It then gained more than 225 percent in 23 months.

NETFLIX—2009

Netflix bottomed in October 2008; the S&P 500 Index didn't bottom until March 2009. In Figure 7-5, notice that while the S&P 500 index made a new low, Netflix shot up 125 percent. This put the stock in a Stage 2 uptrend. The RS line skyrocketed as well as the RS number reported in IBD. The stock hit my radar at this point, but many investors missed it. The reason is that as the market indexes turned up and rallied for several months, Netflix corrected 27 percent and then went sideways for 27 weeks. That was just long enough to wear out most amateur investors. If you look at the RS line, it appears that the stock was underperforming the market—and it was, temporarily. However, the stock was simply digesting the previous rally and catching its breath. To the trained eye, Netflix was mapping out a perfect VCP opportunity and getting ready to make its biggest gain yet. But you needed to look at the big picture and put things into context.

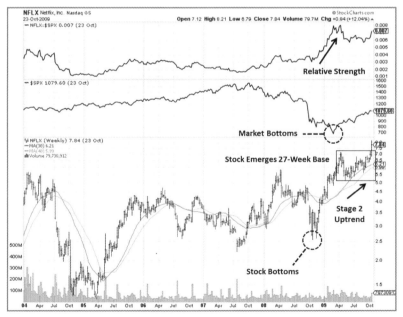

Figure 7-5   Netflix (NFLX) 2009. A soaring relative strength line and a classic VCP set the stage for a 525 percent advance in 21 months.

Leaders don't necessarily emerge right off the market low. Some break out a bit earlier, some right around the time the market bottoms, and, as in the case of Netflix, some emerge several months after the absolute low is established.

After Netflix emerged from a VCP, the stock advanced more than 500 percent in just 21 months. From March 2009 through December 2010, Netflix reported eight consecutive quarters of sales increases; earnings averaged 45 percent. As noted earlier, from the point at which Netflix went public, its stock price increased more than 3,400 percent, while during the same period, Blockbuster's stock lost 99 percent of its value and eventually went bust.

NETFLIX VS. BLOCKBUSTER

Netflix is a very interesting case study. In 2002, within 15 trading days of each other, Netflix went public and Blockbuster Video's stock topped out permanently. With Blockbuster plagued with declining sales and a stock price of just $0.13 (down from $18.00), Netflix with its online offerings was on the verge of taking complete control of the video rental space, edging out the "brick-and-mortar" industry.

On March 18, 2009, just seven days after the Nasdaq Composite traded at its bear market low, and only 10 days after the Dow traded at its bear market low of 6,469, Netflix hit an all-time high (Figure 7-6). Only 17 trading days later, Netflix's stock price was up 20 percent. Earnings in the most recent three quarters were impressive: up 36 percent, 38 percent, and 58 percent, respectively. With such strong performance out of the gate, this was hardly a stock you would want to sell and take profits on.

In October 2009, I was buying Netflix shares based on a well–defined VCP pattern. Netflix was trading at 32x earnings, while Blockbuster traded at just 2x earnings. I avoided the "cheap" shares of Blockbuster and instead bought the much more "expensive" Netflix shares.

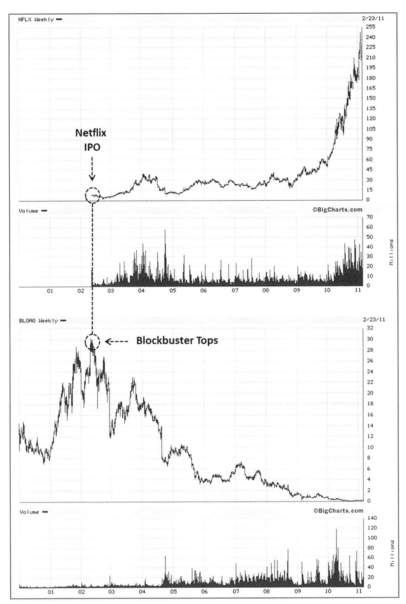

Figure 7-6　Netflix (NFLX) vs. Blockbuster Video (BLOAQ) 2002—2011.
The Netflix IPO coincided with Blockbuster's ultimate top.

Michael Kors vs. Coach

An industry group is usually dominated by one, two, or possibly three companies. Very often a strong competitor is vying for the industry leader's customers. Coca-Cola's archrival was Pepsi. Starbucks and Dunkin' Donuts compete for coffee drinkers, and the home improvement market is split mainly between Home Depot and Lowe's.

Just as it was no coincidence that Blockbuster Video topped when Netflix went public, accessories maker Coach topped right around the time Michael Kors (KORS) went public (Figure 7-7). The reason is simple: competition emerges and takes market share, or a fad fades while a new one emerges. The top rival is always waiting to move in on the leader's action. This is why you should always track and pay attention to the two or three top stocks in an industry group.

Leaders change as new competitors emerge. America Online was the clear leader in the Internet market until the search engine Yahoo! moved into the top slot. Google, a direct competitor to Yahoo!, then went public and is now considered the number one powerhouse in search engines.

A top competitor may not be the superior company or have superior products compared with the true market leader. It could be in the right place at the right time, or perhaps the leader stumbles. Or, as in the fickle retail market, fads change.

Figure 7-7 Michael Kors (KORS) vs. Coach (COH) 2012–2014. A top competitor emerges as an old leader weakens.

Wal-Mart—(WMT) 1981

Back in 1981, Wal-Mart (WMT) was a small, fast-growing company that few were familiar with. On some days, the stock traded only 40,000 or 50,000 shares. Can you imagine? Today, Wal-Mart trades as much as 35 million shares in a single day! During a treacherous bear market decline in the early 1980s, shares of Wal-Mart held up well. The stock was so strong, each time the market indexes experienced a countertrend rally, its price broke out of a base and tried to advance right off the market lows (Figure 7-8). This is the kind of strength leaders display cycle after cycle, year after year. It's a timeless principle; you simply can't hide such a drastic divergence.

Figure 7-8   Wal-Mart Stores (WMT) 1981–1982. +360 percent in 21 months.

APPLE COMPUTER—2004

Leaders in one cycle rarely lead in the next cycle. However, some stocks can emerge late in a bull market and then lead during the next cycle. The thing to look for is how well the stock holds up during a bear market or good-size correction. Apple Computer (AAPL) is a good example (Figure 7-9). The stock set up and emerged from a base in March 2004, right around the time the general market was topping and about to enter a correction. The stock was so strong, however, that each time the general market hit a new low, Apple's shares made a higher low and built another base. Even if you missed the first buy point, you still had two more chances, including one textbook buy point that occurred right off the market low. But if you were focused on the popular indexes and not the leading stocks, you would surely have missed this wonderful opportunity.

Figure 7-9   Apple (AAPL) 2004. Apple presented multiple buying opportunities. The stock rose 125 percent in six months.

WHICH LEADERS SHOULD YOU BUY FIRST?

As you shift into buying gear, the question becomes which stocks should you buy first. It's simple: buy in order of strength. Coming off a market low, I like to buy in order of breakout. The best selections in your lineup will be the first to burst forth and emerge from a proper buy point. The ones that act the strongest are generally the best choices. **Ultimately, opinions mean nothing compared with the wisdom and verdict of the market. Let the strength of the market, not your personal opinion, tell you where to put your money.** The stocks that emerge first and with the greatest power in the early stage of a new bull market, or at the tail end of a correction, are generally the best candidates for superperformance. By the time the market bottoms, though, you could have missed some of the best names if you don't get the first movers advantage.

I can't tell you which stock on my watch list will be my next trade. Out of 5, 6, or 10 names, I don't cheer for one over the other like it was a horse race. In other words, I don't play favorites. Having a favorite means that I "like" a company and I'm willing to wait for it to emerge, while other names—companies that I may not be as familiar with or don't like as much—set up exactly according to my criteria and trigger buy points. Why would I wait for some stock to make a move when other stocks are on the move and meet the correct criteria? It happens all the time. Usually, it's because you have a favorite name for personal reasons; you like the company's status or you're fond of a particular product. Often it's because you want to own a familiar name, and avoid the one you never heard of.

Instead, I let the market tell me where to put my money. I'm looking to get a first-mover advantage, buying the stocks that break out first. I embrace new names instead of avoiding them. Most big winners are companies that just went public within 8 or 10 years. Those early moves often turn out to be the true market leaders, while the stocks that lag often never get out of the gate.

You might have 10 stocks that eventually meet your criteria. But the ones that start to move first are "telling" you where to put your money. Are you going to argue with the market and pass over a perfect setup for some subjective reason or whim? Or are you going to bend your will to that of the market, and trade the opportunities as they come to you?

The stock that is your "favorite" might emerge two or three days later. Or it may never complete the setup or fail to rally. Don't let yourself miss out on perfectly good opportunities because you have a favorite; instead, buy in order of breakout. When you evolve to the point of always being patient and only taking quality trades, that means you've decided that you're not in it for action, but to make money. You're a pro.

THE LOCKOUT RALLY

During the first few months of a new bull market you should see multiple waves of stocks emerging into new high ground. General market pullbacks will be minimal, usually contained to just a few percent from peak to trough. Many inexperienced investors are unwilling to buy during the initial leg of a new powerful bull market because the market appears to be overbought.

Typically, the early phase of a move off an important bottom has the characteristics of a lockout rally. During this lockout period, investors wait for an opportunity to enter the market on a pullback, but that pullback never comes. Instead, demand is so strong that the market moves steadily higher, ignoring overbought readings. As a result, investors are essentially locked out of the market. **If the major market indexes ignore an extremely overbought condition after a bear market decline or correction, and your list of leaders expands, this should be viewed as a sign of strength.** To determine if the rally is real, up days should be accompanied by increased volume, whereas down days should be on lower overall market volume. More important, the price action of leading stocks should be studied to determine if there are stocks emerging from sound, buyable bases and if there's a proliferation of names.

Additional confirmation is given when the list of stocks making new 52-week highs outpaces the new 52-week low list and starts to expand significantly. At this point, you should raise your exposure in accordance with your trading criteria on a stock-by-stock basis. As the adage goes, "It's a market of stocks, not a stock market." In the early stages of a market-bottom rally it's critical to focus on leading stocks if your goal is to latch on to big winners. Sometimes you will be early. Stick with a stop-loss discipline. If the rally is real, the majority of leading stocks will hold up well, and you will have to make only a few adjustments. When you see signs of a lockout rally, look for stocks in sound price structures and buy them as they emerge through proper pivot points.

The 3-C Pattern

The *cup completion cheat*, or 3-C, is a continuation pattern. It's called a "cheat" because at one time I considered it to be an earlier entry than the optimal buy point, so I would say "I'm cheating." Today, I would say that it is the earliest point at which you should attempt to buy any stock. Some stocks form a "low" cheat, and some form the cheat near the middle of the cup or saucer that precedes it. The key is to recognize when the stock has bottomed and identify when the start of a new uptrend is under way, in sync with the primary Stage 2 longer-term uptrend. The cheat trade gives you an actionable pivot point to time a stock's upturn while increasing your odds of success.

A valid cheat area should exhibit a contraction in volume and tightness in price. This pause presents an opportunity to enter the trade at the earliest point, although not always with your entire position. However, you can lower your average cost basis by exploiting cheat areas to scale into trades. Once the stock trades above the high of the pause or pivot point, it has made what I call the turn. This indicates the stock has probably made its low and will resume the longer-term Stage 2 primary trend.

The cheat setup has the same qualifications as the classic cup with handle, because it's simply the cup portion being completed. When a handle forms, it usually occurs in the upper third of the cup. If it forms in the middle third or just below the halfway point, you could get more than one buy point. To qualify, the stock should have already moved up by at least 25 to 100 percent—and in some cases by 200 or 300 percent—during the previous 3 to 36 months of trading. The stock also should be trading above its upwardly trending 200-day moving average (provided that 200 days of trading in the stock has occurred). The pattern can form in as few as 3 weeks to as many as 45 weeks (most are 7 to 25 weeks in duration). The correction from peak to low point varies from 15 or 20 percent to 35 or 40 percent in some cases, and as much as 50 percent, depending on the general market conditions. Corrections in excess of 60 percent are usually too deep and are extremely prone to failure. It is common for a cheat setup to develop during a general market correction. The most powerful stocks will rally off this pattern just as the general market averages turn up from a correction or at least close to the same time (Figure 7-10).

Figure 7-10   Humana (HUM) 1978. Stock emerged from 3-C pattern just days after the Dow made its low. The stock advanced 1,000 percent in 38 months. Note the difference between the 200-day moving average lines; the market is trading below a declining line, while Humana is trading above a rising line.

THE "CHEAT" EXPLAINED

Following are the four steps to a stock turning up through the cheat area (see Figures 7-11 through 7-13):

1. Downtrend. The stock will experience an intermediate-term price correction that takes place within the context of a longer-term Stage 2 uptrend. This leg down can happen over several weeks or months. It is normal to experience large price spikes along the downtrend on increased volume.

2. Uptrend. The price will attempt to rally and break its downtrend. You do not want to buy just yet. It's too early because the price and volume lack the necessary confirmation that the stock has bottomed and entered a new uptrend. The price will start to run up the right side, usually recouping about one-third to one-half its previous decline. However, overhead supply created during the intermediate downtrend will typically be strong enough to stall the price advance and create a pause or pullback.

3. Pause. The stock will pause over a number of days or weeks and form a plateau area (the cheat), which should be contained within 5 percent to 10 percent from high point to low point. The optimum situation is to have the cheat drift down to where the price drops below a prior low point, creating a shakeout—exactly what you'd want to see during the formation of a handle in a cup-with-handle pattern. At this point, the stock is set up and ready to be purchased as it moves above the high of the pause. A typical sign that indicates that the stock is ready to break out is when volume dries up dramatically, accompanied by tightness in price.

4. Breakout. As the stock rallies above the high of the plateau area, you place your buy order. The stock is now deemed to have made the turn, meaning that it probably has put in its low, and the intermediate-term trend is now up and back in sync with the longer-term Stage 2 primary trend.

Figure 7-11   Cirrus Logic (CRUS) 2010. +162 percent in four months from a classic 3-C (cup completion cheat) pattern.

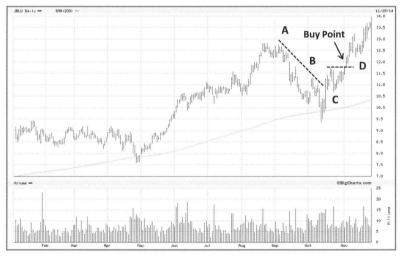

Figure 7-12   JetBlue Airways (JBLU) 2014. The stock emerged from a 3-C pattern (D), and then advanced 130 percent in 11 months.

Figure 7-13   Maxygen (MAXY) 2000. After going public in December 1999, Maxygen emerged from a 3-C in February 2000. It shot up 100 percent in just 14 days.

Chart courtesy of Interactive Data

THE "LOW CHEAT"

The low cheat forms in the lower third of the base. It's riskier to buy in the lower third of the base than in the middle third (the classic cheat area) or the upper third (from the handle). But if you get it right, the profit potential is even greater because you're getting in at a lower price. As stated earlier, I will often start a position at a low cheat and then add as it forms additional pivot points at progressively higher prices. This is how you can scale into a name and lower your average cost.

I like to use the low cheat for larger cap names, and in some cases new issues that recently went public. The low cheat can work for IPOs that don't spend much time trading below their IPO price and don't correct too excessively. It's best if the stock holds above the IPO price. Some can briefly undercut the low, creating a shakeout, and still work. The basing period after the IPO should be at least 10 days. As with any base, you want to avoid buying into heavy overhead supply and a steep ladder of trapped buyers.

For example, Google went public in August 2004. After a brief run-up, the stock corrected and formed a low cheat over in 14 days. As Figure 7-14 demonstrates, the key to the low cheat is the same as any other buy point—tightness in price accompanied by a selling vacuum. Before I buy, I also like to see some inside days on very low volume, another sign that supply coming to market has slowed to a trickle and the line of least resistance is forming.

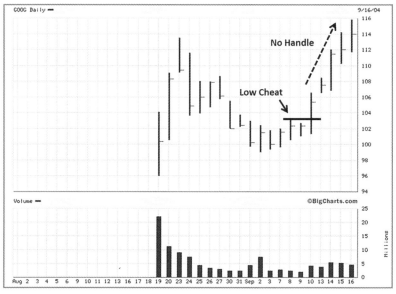

Figure 7-14   Google (GOOG) came public in 2004. Stock emerged from a low cheat and then soared 625 percent in 40 months.

In December 2013, Twitter set up almost identically as Google did a decade earlier (Figure 7-15). The Twitter base formed in 19 days. Although Twitter didn't go on to make the huge gains Google did, the low cheat provided a great trading opportunity; the stock ran up 77 percent in just 16 days.

Another example is Apple Computer, which emerged from a low cheat in August 2004 (Figure 7-16). The stock gapped up sharply on huge volume in July, and then came back to fill the gap on relatively low volume in August. The pivot point or low cheat provided a low-risk entry point—one that was obvious given the large gap upward and low-volume pullback. If the stock had continued lower, it would become obvious that something was wrong, providing a very clear-cut exit point.

Figure 7-15   Twitter (TWTR) 2015. Stock made a quick move from a low cheat.

Figure 7-16   Apple (AAPL) 2004. Stock formed a low cheat after a sharp gap upward on huge volume, followed by a low-volume pullback.

The "Dream Pattern"

In the 1960s, William L. Jiler wrote *How Charts Can Help You in the Stock Market*, a book that was way ahead of its time and to this day still has valuable findings. I would put it on the must-read list for anyone interested in using charts to improve their performance in the stock market. Jiler was the first to highlight the saucer-with-platform pattern, which later became popularized as the cup-with-handle pattern. Without a doubt, this pattern is the most repeatable and reliable price structure that superperformance stocks trace out before they advance dramatically in price.

Jiler refers to the saucer pattern as a "dream pattern," citing its ease of recognition and reliability. Although I agree with Jiler, the pattern is prone to misinterpretation; however, the VCP concept and some education about volume can quickly clear up poor analysis and lead you to find the next big superperformer. As was mentioned above, volatility contraction is a key characteristic of constructive price behavior within all patterns including this one.

In 1990, amidst soaring oil prices and the United States on the brink of war with Iraq, the stock market entered a brutal bear market. Almost everyone thought the market was going to go much lower. But I noticed a huge number of stocks forming large 3-C patterns and the cup-with-handle pattern. Many would form a cheat area, run up a bit, and then form a handle. While the major market indexes were all trading below their 200-day moving averages, every one of these stocks were above their own 200-day lines and 50-day lines, and each had an RS number in the mid- to high 90s.

Fortunately for me, my discipline won over my emotions. Based on my observations of the charts, I started buying stocks in October 1990, and as my trades performed favorably, I accelerated my buying into January 1991. Coincidentally, just after I bought several names emerging from these well-formed correction patterns, *Investors Business Daily* ran the headline "Cup with Handles Proliferate" and published charts of a handful of stocks that had or were about to emerge from cup-with-handle patterns. The rest is history. One of the greatest bull markets in history unleashed in January 1991 (right on the day the United States attacked Iraq). By letting the charts, and not my emotions guide me, I owned some of the most powerful market leaders that went on to make legendary returns. Many of these stocks went on to become household names, such as Microsoft, Amgen, Home Depot, Dell Computer, Cisco Systems, and others (Figures 7-17 and 7-18). At the time, though, few people had heard of these companies; they were all relatively small unknown stocks.

Figure 7-17   Microsoft (MSFT) 1989–1990. +5,100 percent in nine years.

Figure 7-18   Home Depot (HD) 1990. Stock emerged from a classic cup-with-handle pattern.

THE DOUBLE BOTTOM

The double bottom is a structure that forms a "W" and undercuts, or in some cases tests, a previous low within the base. I prefer an undercut, because it tends to shake out more weak holders. I also want to see a pause or pivot point on the right side of the base, as with all the base structures I trade. The double bottom could set a cheat area and/or a handle just like the other patterns discussed. Structures that run straight up off the lows with no cheat or handle are more prone to failure.

This pattern can also develop soon after an IPO as a primary base or second stage base (see Figure 7-19): in April 2003, Dick's Sporting Goods emerged from a post-IPO double bottom, around the time the general market was bottoming.

Figure 7-19   Dick's Sporting Goods (DKS) 2002–2003. +200 percent in 15 months from a double bottom.

THE POWER PLAY

Rounding out our discussion here is the power play, also referred to as the high tight flag. This is one of the most important and profitable set-ups to learn—and one of the most misinterpreted among all the technical patterns. If you get it right, though, it can be one of the most profitable. The power play is what I call a velocity pattern for two reasons. First, it takes a great deal of momentum to qualify as a power play; in fact, the first requirement is a sharp price thrust upward. Second, these setups can move up fast in the shortest time, and often they signal a dramatic shift in the prospects of a company. The rapid price run-up could be induced by a major news development such as an FDA drug approval, litigation resolution, a new product or service announcement, or even an earnings report; it can also occur on no news at all. Some of the best trades from this setup can develop as unexplained strength. Therefore, this is the type of situation I will enter even with a dearth of fundamentals. It doesn't mean that improving fundamentals don't exist; very often they do. However, with the power play, the stock is exhibiting so much strength, it's telling you that something is going on regardless of what the current earnings and sales show.

Although I don't demand that a power play have fundamentals on the table, I do require the same VCP characteristics that I do with all the other setups. Even the power play must go through a proper digestion of supply and demand. With a power play, you should look for tight weekly closes over three to six weeks.

To qualify as a power play, the following criteria must be met:

• An explosive price move on huge volume that propels the stock price up 100 percent or more within eight weeks. Stocks that have already made a huge gain coming off a late-stage base usually don't qualify. The best power plays are stocks that were quiet in Stage 1 and then suddenly explode.

• Following the explosive move, the stock price moves sideways in a relatively tight range, not correcting more than 20 percent (some lower-priced stocks can correct as much as 25 percent) over a period of three to six weeks (some can emerge after only 10 or 12 days).

• If the correction in the base, from high to low, does not exceed 10 percent, it is not necessary to see price tightening in the form of a volatility contraction, because the price is already tight enough.

On February 4, 2010—the day the Nasdaq Composite Index was hitting a new low—I purchased Pharmacyclics Inc. (PCYC) and also recommended it to our Minervini Private Access clients (Figure 7-20). Over the next 48 trading days, Pharmacyclics advanced 90 percent, during which time the Nasdaq rallied only about 18 percent. The 90 percent advance proved to be only the beginning; the stock advanced 2,600 percent in 43 months, a clear example of market leadership.

Knowing which stocks to buy—when and where—takes a well-thought-out plan, executed without emotion. Fortunately, there are rules

Figure 7-20   Pharmacyclics (PCYC) 2010.

and criteria to guide these decisions. While it takes time and discipline to learn how to identify the best stock candidates and pinpoint optimal buy points, for those of you who are willing to commit to learning and applying the correct criteria, well-timed purchases will put you on the road to superperformance.

POSITION SIZING FOR OPTIMAL RESULTS

In a lecture to his students at a 1991 retreat in Hawaii, fellow Market Wizard Ed Seykota said that once you know the expectancy of your system, the most important question a trader can ask is, "How much should I invest?" One of the most frequent questions I'm asked is how to determine the correct position size per trade. Ultimately, this becomes a discussion of how many stocks to hold in a portfolio. While it's true that the more concentrated your portfolio, the bigger gains you can make in a shorter time, it depends on whether things go your way. The first rule is to never put your entire account into just one stock; that would be taking too much risk. If you have hopes of making a short-term killing by risking it all, you're liable to be the one killed! If there's even a 1 percent chance of ruin, it's an unacceptable risk. Remember, you're not going to make just one trade. Even if there's a 1-in-100 chance of a catastrophe, that misfortune becomes a certainty, because you're going to make at least 100 trades, and probably thousands of trades, during your lifetime. Each time you risk it all, you are essentially tempting fate.

On the other hand, if you want to achieve superperformance, diversifying your portfolio too much is counterproductive. Diversification is a tactic used to distribute investments among different securities to limit losses in the event of a decline in a particular security or industry. The strategy relies on the average security having a profitable expected value. Diversification also provides some psychological benefits to single-instrument trading since some of the short-term variation in one instrument may cancel out that from another instrument, resulting in an overall smoothing of short-term portfolio volatility.

Your goal should be optimal position sizing. The size of your position should be determined by how much equity you stand to lose if a trade goes against you. Let's say you have a $100,000 portfolio and you put 50 percent ($50,000) into one position. With a 10 percent stop, you cap your loss at $5,000. But that's 5 percent of the total equity of your account—and that's too much risk. If you were to suffer a string of such losses, you would put yourself at risk of ruin. **Instead of arbitrarily picking a number, your maximum risk should be no more than 1.25 to 2.5 percent of your equity on any one trade.** The less experienced you are, the less risk you should take on because you are at or near the bottom of the learning curve and more prone to mistakes and losses.

To understand more about how position size affects your risk, let's say you have a $100,000 portfolio and commit $25,000 (25 percent of your account) to one stock. With a 10 percent stop, you're putting $2,500 of equity at risk if you lose on that trade—or 2.5 percent of total equity. That's at the high end of the range for ideal exposure. If you want to lower your exposure you could tighten your stop to 5 percent, putting only $1,250 or 1.25 percent of equity at risk. If you wanted to keep your 10 percent stop, your only other choice to reduce equity risk would be to cut down the position size to $12,500 (12.5 percent of your account), thus reaching $1,250 or 1.25 percent of equity at risk.

Either your stop moves or your position size moves. One or the other must be adjusted to dial in the correct amount of risk. For argument's sake, if you wanted to be very aggressive and put 50 percent of your account into one position, you would need to use a 5 percent stop to contain your risk as a percentage of equity to 2.50 percent. But the tighter your stop, the more likely you are to get stopped out. The key is to find a balance between an acceptable position size and a stop that allows the stock's price to fluctuate normally without choking off the trade. This is known as backing into risk.

When you back into risk, you are approaching the trade risk-first, which should always be your line of thinking. If you adhere to my position sizing guidelines below, you will never take on too much risk per position. Then it's up to you if you want to take less or more risk, up to the maximum level (Figure 8-1).

Position Sizing Using $100,000 Portfolio

1.25% risk of total equity 10% stop	1.25% risk of total equity 5% stop	1.25% risk of total equity 2.5% stop
1.25% = $1,250 100K x 12.5% =$12,500 $12,500 x 10% = $1,250	1.25% = $1,250 100K x 25% = $25,000 $25,000 x 5% = $1,250	1.25% = $1,250 100K x 50% = $50,000 $50,000 x 2.5% = $1,250
12.5% POSITION	**25% POSITION**	**50% POSITION**

Figure 8-1   Examples of position sizing with various levels of risk.

Position Sizing Guidelines

- 1.25–2.50 percent risk of total equity
- 10 percent maximum stop
- Losses should average no more than 5–6 percent
- Never take a position larger than 50 percent
- Shoot for optimal 20–25 percent positions in the best names
- No more than 10–12 stocks total (16–20 for larger professional portfolios)

Depending on the size of your portfolio and your risk tolerance, you should typically have between 4 and 8 stocks and for large portfolios maybe as many as 10 or 12 stocks. This will provide sufficient diversification but not too much. There is no need to own more than 20 names, which would represent a 5 percent position size per position if they were equally weighted.

Ideally, I like to concentrate my capital in the best names, for example, devoting 20 to 25 percent of my portfolio in each of my top four or five stock picks. But it doesn't always work like that. Often, I start with a much smaller position, 5 to 10 percent of my portfolio, so that my risk is less until a stock can prove itself. If the stock performs as I had hoped, I will increase my position size accordingly or add additional names as they meet my buy criteria.

When I am fully invested with a good portion of my account in four or five of the best stocks, I don't close my eyes to everything else. I constantly evaluate my holdings to see which stocks are performing the best, and if any new names are emerging from my watch list. If I have a stellar performer in my portfolio, I want to give that stock time and room to run. But if a stock is not appreciating in a timely manner or looks like it's coming to the end of its run, it's probably time to reallocate into a more promising candidate.

Think of your portfolio like a garden. You pull the weeds and water the flowers—nurturing what you want to grow and getting rid of anything unwanted that's only depleting resources. You'll find that some of the stocks in your portfolio aren't the "flowers" you had hoped they'd be. Instead, they're looking more weed-like. This doesn't mean a stock has hit your stop; it may just be sitting there, doing not much of anything. As time goes on, you must consider how your money could be better invested in something that is poised to move.

THE TWO-FOR-ONE RULE

If out of six stocks, four are doing well, but two are mediocre or poor performers, it's probably time to reallocate your capital. To do so, you don't have to dump the two lackluster performers completely. Instead, you can reduce your positions in them. For example, **you can sell half your position in each of the two underperforming stocks and then buy a full position in the more promising candidate. The capital you raised from selling the two half positions finances your new full position.**

Let's say you hold five stocks, each accounting for 20 percent of your portfolio. If Company A and Company B are the weakest performers, you can reduce those holdings by half, from 20 percent to 10 percent of your total equity. The combined 20 percent (10 percent each from A and B) then can be invested in another stock. By reallocating your capital, you are sowing "new seed" to refurbish your garden and keep it growing.

Don't Sell Leaders Too Quickly

Keeping some of your position after a run-up is especially important if it's the beginning of a new bull market and you've bought stocks that have been leading the move. You don't want to sell too quickly just because there are profits and you want to buy something else. **Sometimes the best stock to buy is the one you already own.** You can sell a portion of the strong performers, take some profits, and reinvest in another promising name. The remainder of your original position, meanwhile, is allowed to keep growing as you try to get a bigger move from the name.

At the start of a new bull market, in particular, there could be plenty of upside potential, even for stocks that have already made strong advances. **At the beginning of a new bull market, you don't want to give up your entire position in a leader.** The stocks that come out of the gate the strongest in a new market uptrend are often the best performers going forward. I usually will hold 25 to 50 percent of my original position for a larger move in these strong leaders.

Don't "Di-worsify"

As you sell some of your stocks and reallocate capital into others, you don't want to spread yourself so thin that you're overly diversified. That's not diversification; I call it "di-worsification." Not only is it hard to keep track of a large number stocks, but your positions are going to be small, which will undermine the potential to get superperformance out of a really big winner. Bottom line: **you will never achieve superperformance if you overly diversify and rely on diversification for protection.** It's better to learn how to concentrate your buys in the best names precisely at the right time and then protect yourself with the use of intelligent stop-loss placement.

In the other extreme, one of the big dangers with overconcentration—such as having 75 or even 100 percent of your portfolio in one stock—is the potentially disastrous exposure to a downside event. It may be rare for a stock to get into trouble suddenly and gap down huge, say 50 percent in one day, but it does happen. When a stock gaps down so severely, your 5 or 10 percent stop is worthless, because the stock traded through that level and you will be sold out at the next best price. There is nothing but dead air between where the stock closed the night before and where it opens the next morning. Your position is now worth 50 percent less! You may say, "I'll just wait for it to come back and sell it then," but you have no assurance that it will come back, which adds additional risk. If a stock suffers a 50 percent decline and you committed 80 percent of your portfolio to that one stock, you've just lost 40 percent of your equity. That is going to take a lot of time and much hard work to make it up, just to get back to breakeven.

If you adhere to my position sizing guidelines and only risk 1.25 to 2.50 percent of your equity on any one trade, you will never have to worry about a stock wiping you out. Even if you take a 25 percent position and the stock drops 50 percent, you would only suffer a 12.5 percent loss. Admittedly, that would be a serious hit to your equity curve, but recoverable.

It bears repeating: the secret to successful trading is to make consistent profits that, when strung together, make for a very strong return. That happens by being tactical and smart, not by gambling with too much size and taking on too much risk, because even one loss of that magnitude may be too big to recover from.

That's why, as I've said before, it's so important to know the truth about your trading with statistics such as your average loss, average gain, and your batting average. Facing these numbers isn't about your ego or making yourself feel good or bad about your past performance. You want to deal with reality, especially when it comes to position sizing. **Use the math of your results as a tool, and hone your edge by calculating the amount of risk you should be taking based on your own performance.**

An important factor in determining the amount of equity you risk per trade is your average loss. Let's assume your average loss—not your largest or smallest loss, but the average—runs at 5 percent. Further, let's assume your "batting average" of wins versus losses is 50 percent, meaning for every two trades you win one and lose one. And, your average gain is 10 percent. With these statistics, calculating your position size becomes a mathematical equation. You can use "Optimal F" or its cousin, the Kelly Formula, to calculate optimal position sizing.

If you venture into the math of optimal position sizing, you will learn that as a 2:1 trader, mathematically, your optimal position size should be 25 percent (four stocks divided equally). As a result, a stock that is a big winner will make a real contribution to your portfolio. In keeping track of 4, 5, or 6 companies, it is much easier to know a lot about each name than it is to follow and track 15 or 20 companies. If you're holding a large number of positions, it's going to be difficult to raise cash and move quickly when the market turns against you. Instead of spreading yourself all over the place in a feeble attempt to mitigate risk through diversification, concentrate your capital in the very best stocks—a relatively small group.

To leave you with some further perspective on this topic, I have had many periods in which I put my entire account in just four or five names. This of course corresponds with some of my most profitable periods. Yes, there is risk, but you can mitigate that risk with proper position sizing balanced with a stop-loss that keeps you in the range of my position sizing guidelines. If you are strict with your selection criteria and choose the best stocks for your portfolio, it should be difficult to find a lot of names that are worthy to be included among your elite group. Remember, diversification does not protect you from losses, and too much concentration will put you at risk of ruin. Optimal position sizing is the goal.

WHEN TO SELL AND NAIL DOWN PROFITS

This section is without a doubt one of the most eagerly awaited discussions in this new book: when and how to sell. When I wrote *Trade Like a Stock Market Wizard: How to Achieve Superperformance in Any Market*, I had a lot of content to cover and limited room, space-wise. As a result, I had to make some hard choices about which topics to explore in greatest detail. This section addresses one of those areas that was only summarized in my first book. For that reason, readers should consider my books to be a "multi-volume set."

Previously, we discussed selling in the context of cutting your losses. In Section 1, we addressed "violations" that could tip you off when to sell before your stop is hit based on abnormal stock price activity soon after a buy point is triggered. Selling out of a profitable position after a stock has moved in your favor and has made a decent gain is an entirely separate topic. In this section, we will examine how and where to nail down your profits.

When I first started trading, I devoted almost all my energy to learning how and when to buy. Most of my effort was spent on fundamental and technical analysis, and I honed my selection criteria until I gained the confidence that I could put my hard-earned capital on the line in a trade. The next challenge was learning how to cut my losses and mitigate risk without fail. Once my money was on the line in a stock trade, I was exposed to risk of principal. I had to learn how to manage that risk effectively to protect my account. Finally, I started making some decent profits. That's when I discovered a hole in my trading plan. I had spent so much time on stock selection—really gaining an edge when it came to buying—I didn't have a clue as to when I should sell and how to handle a big winner.

It never occurred to me that this would be a problem. I figured that once I finally had a decent profit in a stock, I'd just sell it. But the better my selection criteria became and the more profitable trades I had, the more pressure I experienced with these profits. This is often surprising for people, because the intuitive assumption is that a profit would alleviate the pressure. If you have a profit, you should be happy, right? As with everything in trading, selling brings its own emotional pressures. Selling at a profit is not as easy as it looks—and it's fraught with emotions. And that is where this discussion is going to start.

THE EMOTIONS OF SELLING AT A PROFIT

One of the most indecisive moments in trading is when to sell. Sell too soon and you fear losing out on future profits. Sell too late and you regret giving back your profits. Two emotions—fear and regret—lead to indecisiveness: *Should I sell? Should I hold? What if I sell too soon—or too late?* These "sell-side" fears are no different from what you felt before you bought the stock: *Should I buy now? Should I have bought yesterday? Should I wait longer?*

The best—in fact, the only—way to control these emotions and keep them from undermining your success is with sound trading rules. Otherwise, you're always going to get caught in the crossfire of your own excitement and doubt.

There are two basic scenarios in which to sell. The first is to sell into strength while the stock is moving in the direction of your trade and buyers are plentiful. You have a position in a stock that's doing great, and you use that strength to sell into. This is how pros sell, especially if they have a sizable position to unload. When you have a large amount of stock to sell, and liquidity is an issue, you get out when you can, not necessarily when you want.

Most individual traders don't have that problem; however, you still want to learn how to sell into strength. Why? Because you don't want to give a stock the chance to break and give back a large portion of your profits. You may want to wait until the signs are clear that a stock should be sold based on a weakening trend. But if you do, it usually turns out that you would have been better off selling earlier, into strength, as it will often turn out to be a more favorable price.

The second scenario is selling into weakness. Your stock made a good run at first, but now the price action is weakening, and you need to protect your gains as the stock reverses direction. This can happen unexpectedly requiring, in many cases, a very swift response.

Both plans start with an "aerial view."

ALWAYS PUT THE CHART INTO PERSPECTIVE

In my first book, I spent a great deal of time explaining how I look at trading from the "aerial" view down to the microscopic. This is how I identify stocks to trade, and then pinpoint my entry. I start with the long-term trend, which I always want to be in my favor, and then the current chart pattern and the underlying fundamentals. After that, I get very surgical and precise, studying the last few days of price and volume action. All this gives me the specific point for entering a trade.

When it comes to selling, it's a similar process: **You need to have some perspective, starting with the big picture. From an aerial view, you begin to understand the context of the current price action. Without this perspective, you run a high risk of becoming victim of your fears and emotions.** You'll say to yourself, "What if I sell now and it's too soon?" Or, you'll wait for no particular reason other than trying to squeeze out every dime of profit, and regret it later: "Oh, why didn't I sell back then?" Fear and regret, as I said before, are the driving emotions of trading.

In addition to looking at the long-term trend and the current chart pattern, you need to have some guidelines and rules based on your own personal math. These objectives, while not perfect every time, at least give you some idea of where you should nail down profits to maintain an edge.

For example, let's say you set an 8 percent stop-loss to control your risk (you buy a stock at $100 a share and place your stop at $92). If the stock goes up 5 or 6 percent—in this example to $105 or $106 a share—do you sell? For a lot of people, the answer is yes. Why? Because they are fearful; with a small profit to capture they're happy to sell. They grab a 5- or 6-point gain, not even thinking that the reward/risk is unfavorable. But why would you risk 8 percent to make only 5 or 6 percent? That's a perfect example of selling too soon without any real justification and a great recipe for having regrets.

Or consider the example of setting an 8 percent stop, which the stock never goes near. Instead, it rises from $100 to $105, and then $110 and then $125. Is it time to sell? Without any rules or rationale, you might get complacent and convince yourself that this $100 stock is going to $150—maybe even $200. Once again, fear is driving you—this time, fear of missing out on an opportunity and getting too greedy. You don't want to regret the profit that "could have been" if only you had held on longer. You convince yourself that you're in for the long haul on this one; it's bound to double or triple (again, without perspective or considering the math). Every tick higher is spellbinding, and you can't think about anything other than "how high is up" on this stock.

What you don't realize, however, is that this stock is not starting its first run. In fact, it is in the last stages of a much bigger run-up and is about to come crashing down. The first drop is sharp, from $120 to $108. Now you panic, but you convince yourself that once it goes back up you'll sell. Except the stock doesn't go back up to $120. It keeps going down, while you keep holding on to fading hopes of a reversal to the upside, until you give in and sell at a very small profit or, worse, at a loss.

To speak bluntly, fear can make you stupid. Afraid of losing that first small profit, you sell too soon. And fear that you'll leave money on the table makes you hang on too long. Your ego is tied up in this because you want to be "right," which, ironically, increases your chances of being wrong.

THE BASE COUNT

Knowing when and where to sell requires analysis, just as you did to identify the stock you bought and to pinpoint your entry spot. An important factor that influences the decision to sell is where the stock is within its own cycle. One way to assess this is with the "base count" to help you identify whether the stock is in the early or late stages of its upward move. This matters tremendously because it will help inform your decision about the likelihood of a continued move, or if you should be on the lookout for more specific sell signals.

If a stock is in the earlier stages of an upward price trajectory, you will want to give that stock some time to make a full-scale advance. You could be onto a key leader ready to embark upon a huge move, in which case you'll want to give it time to become a much bigger winner. Or, the market could be in the late stages of a bull market and your stock is in the late stage of its own expansion; the strong move you're seeing is the last gasp before it comes crashing down. **Late-stage stocks need to be treated very differently than early-stage names. But you won't know the difference or where you are in the life cycle of a stock unless you study the charts and learn what to look for.**

Borrowing the explanation from my first book, the movement of a stock's price through the stages of its life cycle resembles the outline of a mountain, from flatlands to the summit and back to the flatlands again. As the mountain rises, there are plateaus; this is where the price ascent stops or rests for a bit. If this were a real mountain, these plateaus would be where climbers would establish base camps to rest and recharge. This is exactly what happens with a stock's price action.

Following a run upward, there is some profit-taking, causing a temporary pullback. This activity causes the stock to decline and build a base—a short-term pause that allows the stock to digest its previous run-up. If the stock is truly in the middle of something significant, and long-term buyers outweigh short-term traders, the longer-term trend will resume.

More than 90 percent of big upward moves emerge from market corrections. That's your golden opportunity to get into stocks that are coming out of their early to midstage bases. After a bear market decline, the initial plateau counts as the first base. When stocks are coming out of bases 1 or 2 following a market correction, that's generally the best time to jump onboard a new trend; bases 3 and 4 can also work, but are later in the cycle and should be treated more as trading opportunities. Bases 5 or 6 are extremely failure prone and should be viewed as opportunities to sell into soon after a price breakout gets extended. Sometimes the later-stage bases can get exciting as stocks can often experience climactic moves during late-stage "blow-off" run-ups. But these are the most difficult periods to sell into because the stock is soaring and appears to have no end in sight.

Keep in mind, the later-stage bases become increasingly obvious, and the more obvious they get, the more people will have piled into the stock. All that are left are potential sellers; this is what I call and some refer to as a "crowded" trade. As they say in the stock market, what's obvious is obviously wrong. As the stock gets crowded, all eyes are on it because it has already made a strong move, and investors have seen the bases work many times in the past. This attracts less-informed investors. The "smart money" that got in early is now looking to exit and lock in profits, and dump the stock into retail buyers' hands. This selling or liquidation takes place on the way up when the stock is making headlines and everyone is excited and happy; that's why it's difficult for most investors to identify.

DECKERS OUTDOOR

Deckers came out of a first-stage base on September 12, 2006; it advanced more than 260 percent in 15 months (Figure 9-1). By December 2008, the stock price had gone through four identifiable bases on a weekly chart. At this point, it had reached a late-stage move, coming out of a fourth base. If you hadn't counted bases, however, you might mistake a late-stage base for an early-stage base. The fifth and final base was noticeably wide and loose, and prone to failure. This was clear-cut evidence that the stock was topping in Stage 3. You should have already been out of the stock by then or selling aggressively once the fifth base failed and the stock started to roll over.

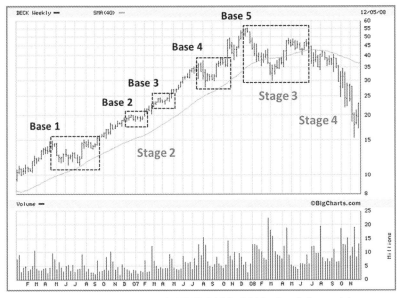

Figure 9-1 Deckers Outdoors (DECK) 2006–2008. Stock formed four distinct bases through its Stage 2 advance before selling off in late 2008 and entering a Stage 4 decline.

P/E EXPANSION

I rarely concern myself with the price-to-earnings (P/E) ratio. The growth stocks I normally buy are already "expensive" for a reason: strong growth. So rather than being scared off by a high P/E, I consider it one of the characteristics of a fast-growing company. In fact, it troubles me more when a stock's P/E is exceptionally low rather than high because it could signal something is seriously wrong.

There is, however, a time when the P/E can be helpful. In addition to base counting, the stock's P/E also can give you some indication as to where a stock is in its life cycle. Specifically, the P/E can tell you whether the run-up is late-stage and further upward momentum is likely to become exhausted. Here's how I use the P/E in conjunction with the base count:

When I buy a stock, I take note of its P/E ratio. Now, let's say this is a position I hold over the next year. During that time, the stock goes through two, three, or four bases—as described, periods of "plateaus" when previous upward surges are digested before the price acceleration continues. When that stock gets to a late-stage base—let's say it's putting in base 4 or 5—I take note of the P/E again and compare it to ratio when I bought it. Or, if I bought a stock during a later-stage base, I'll compare the current P/E to the ratio at the first base at the beginning of the move. If that P/E has doubled or more—say from 20 to 40—I know I must be careful (Figures 9-2 through 9-4). Here's why:

The numerator of the P/E is the stock's current price. The denominator is earnings. With a growth stock, we would expect that the price would be multiples of its earnings because people are buying the stock now in anticipation of future earnings growth. But as a stock becomes more popular—now it's on everybody's radar—the price can get too far ahead of the reality of what the company is actually able to deliver. It is possible, especially in early stages, that the P/E will go down or stay flat even as the price moves higher, because earnings (the denominator) are growing faster than the stock price is accelerating. But when the stock price acceleration gets far ahead of the actual earnings, then you will see P/E expansion.

The absolute value of the P/E is not that important; the comparison is what matters most. **What would concern me is the stock price running ahead of the earnings to the point that the P/E expanded to two or more times what it was at the beginning of a major move—particularly if the stock is also in a late-stage base as determined by a proper base count.** If that's the case, I would start looking closely for specific sell signals.

This same analysis is also extremely helpful in deciding whether you should buy a stock. If you count the number of bases since the stock came out of a correction, say, two years earlier, and you see that it has gone through five consolidation periods, and the P/E has doubled or tripled, you should be very cautious about buying. There may not be much more upside left for the stock.

Figure 9-2   Deckers Outdoors (DECK) 2006–2008.

Figure 9-3   Lumber Liquidators (LL) September 2013.

Figure 9-4   Chipotle Mexican Grill (CMG) October 2012.

The Climax Top

Many leading stocks will top after an accelerated rate of advance or what is commonly described as a climax or blow-off top. The reason big stock moves tend to end like this is because big institutions need buyers to absorb their large blocks of shares. As a result, liquidation takes place on the way up when the price is advancing and there are buyers available, as the stock moves from strong professional hands to weak retail hands. Eventually, the large institutional volume overwhelms the retail appetite, and the stock comes crashing down. If you wait until that happens, you will be late and probably will give back a good portion, if not all, of your profits. It's best to learn how to spot a climax top and sell on the way up. This will help you nail down a sizeable profit and avoid the common mistake of giving back much of what you gained.

After a leading stock has made a healthy advance for many months, the price will accelerate and start to run up at a faster pace and a steeper angle than at any time during the advance. When this occurs, you should sell into the rally and nail down some, if not all, of

your profits. A climax top occurs when the stock price runs up 25 to 50 percent or more over the course of one to three weeks. Some can advance 70 to 80 percent in just 5 or 10 days.

One of the all-time great climax moves occurred in Qualcomm back in the 1990s (Figure 9-5). The stock offered investors two excellent opportunities to sell into strength. The first was an accelerated advance in November 1999 when the stock price shot up 80 percent in just nine days. Then in December the final blow-off lasted just six days when the stock price advanced 73 percent. In just two months Qualcomm's stock price soared 260 percent, and then it topped and fell 88 percent in 2½ years. Amazon followed a similar pattern (Figure 9-6).

Figure 9-5   Qualcomm (QCOM) 1999. Stock staged a climax top. +260% in two months.

Figure 9-6   Amazon.com (AMZN) 1999. Stock topped in epic fashion: it ran up 97 percent in just six days. The stock price then fell 95 percent—from above $100 to $5.51 a share, and took 10 years to get back to its previous level.

SELLING INTO STRENGTH— SPECIFIC THINGS TO WATCH

Let's say the stock you bought some time ago is now in a late stage, as you confirm by counting bases. You can tell by the P/E expansion that the stock appreciation has gotten considerably ahead of the earnings growth. Plus, the stock is a good distance away from its most recent base (it's "extended"). It's time to get more granular and look for very specific sell signals (Figures 9-7 and 9-8).

Start by counting the number of days the stock closed higher (up days) versus how many it closed lower (down days). This is important because during a price run-up you will be especially vulnerable to your emotions. For example, a late-stage rally could transition into a blow-off top when the stock starts running very rapidly and never seems to go down. When you observe the stock going up and up—and you're making more and more money—it's hard to think clearly about selling.

As you count up versus down days, you'll start to see a shift where up days dominate down days. Maybe 6 out of 8 are up days, and then a few weeks later 8 out of 11 are up days. **Look for 70 percent or more up days versus down days over a 7- to 15-day period (example: 7 of 10 days are up).** As a general guideline, once the stock is extended, look for 6 to 10 days of accelerated advance, with only 2 or 3 days being down. At this point, the price is likely to be considerably above the base. Now, you'll want to look for the largest up day and/or the largest daily spread since the beginning of the move. That last blast of upward momentum usually signals that the run is over; very often this occurs within a few days of the top. You also should look for recent exhaustion gaps, another sign the stock could soon come crashing down. When you put all of this together, it's time to start selling aggressively into strength.

Look for the following warnings:

- New highs from late fourth and fifth stage bases
- P/E expansion by twice or more during late-stage price action
- Climax run or blow-off top (price up 25 to 50 percent or more in one to three weeks)
- On extended stocks, 70 percent or more up days versus down days over a 7- to 15-day period
- Once the stock is extended, 6 to 10 days of accelerated advance with all but 2 or 3 days being down

In addition:

- Look for the largest up day since the beginning of a long move during the fast run-up.
- Look for the widest daily spread from high to low.
- Look for recent exhaustion gaps.

Figure 9-7   Tesla Motors (TSLA) 2014. After making a more than ninefold move in 16 months, Tesla Motors experienced a climax run; the stock doubled in just 30 days. During the last 14 days, the stock ran up 51 percent on three gaps; 10 of 14 days were up.

Figure 9-8   Monster Beverage (MNST) 2006. After being up eight out of nine days, the stock experienced several gaps higher, and gained more than 58 percent in eight days.

Look for Signs of Reversal and Heavy Volume

Consider this scenario: A stock confirmed by your base count to be in a late stage has run up 10 of 11 days. As you look for specific sell signals, paying particular attention to the largest up day, you are also on the look-out for the day with the heaviest volume. What is the price action on that day? Does the heavy volume come on a down day? If so, then you are seeing large investors liquidating their positions. At this point, if you haven't sold, you will want to do so soon. Keep in mind, liquidation occurs on the way up. Big investors sell into strength when everything looks great. But that big supply will eventually overwhelm the retail demand; when big institutions want out, a stock can fall very fast and furious. When you see abnormal negative price action relative to the price action during the big advance, look out!

Many times, although not always, there are warnings that occur before a stock has a chance to break. When your stock is extended in price and most days are up days, you'll probably feel complacent. This is when you should calm your emotions and start homing in on specific sell signals that can occur on just one or a few days (Figures 9-9 and 9-10). Those include

- High-volume reversals
- Elevated volume without much price progress—"churning"
- The stock price down on the largest volume since the beginning of the move

Figure 9-9   Green Mountain Coffee Roasters (GMCR) 2007. Classic exhaustive "sell signals" after a large upward move.

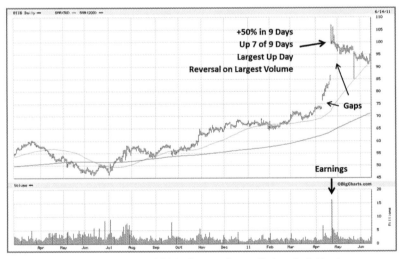

Figure 9-10   Biogen (BIIB) 2011. Converging sell signals following a strong upward run produced enough negatives to stall the stock for six months.

SELLING INTO WEAKNESS

When your stock experiences material weakness, your ego may tell you to hold on. "I'll wait until it snaps back," you think to yourself. But these signals shouldn't be ignored. Once you start seeing warnings that your stock is extended and vulnerable, holding out for more is just exposing yourself to unnecessary risk and potential air pockets (sharp sudden drops in price). The danger is that there's a good chance the stock will come off its highs hard and fast on a surge in volume.

When this occurs, it's a major sell signal, because the big boys are piling out, and you can't fight a tsunami of institutional selling. Sometimes it even happens on "good" news, such as an earnings report. The discrepancy between what appears to be good news and a sharp sell-off often confuses investors. They can't figure out why the stock is down, because in their minds it should be up. As I explained earlier, this may be a case of "differential disclosure."

Before it becomes apparent that the fundamentals of a company have changed, a major break in the stock price could occur on overwhelming volume. **If your stock experiences its largest daily and/or weekly price decline since the beginning of a Stage 2 advance, this is almost always an outright sell signal.** Even if it comes on the heels of a seemingly good earnings report or news item, it's not likely a bargain—don't listen to the company or the media; listen to the stock.

Often before a fundamental problem becomes evident, there will be significant change in price behavior. That change should always be respected even if you don't see any reason for the sudden shift in sentiment. Earnings may still look good; the story may still be intact. However, in most cases, you'll be far better off getting out and asking questions later than waiting to learn the reason why, which often doesn't become apparent until the stock has suffered a large decline.

Whatever you do, don't think that a big break in the stock is now a buying opportunity. Many investors get caught in this trap: A stock they own suddenly declines sharply. Believing that the marketplace must be wrong and that the stock is still a good performer, they decide it's time to buy more. They don't realize that the stock price is down because the big players know (or at least suspect) something is wrong and are getting out; when you see that happen, it's time to exit. This sell signal can occur without warning, or in many cases you will see a multitude of sell violations start to pile up. If you didn't have the courage to sell earlier into strength, then you'd better have the smarts to sell now.

The topping pattern in stocks will not hold true in every single case. For example, stocks won't necessarily have their largest down day on the largest volume. Sometimes the largest down day happens on elevated volume, but it's not the largest volume. Be prepared to notice the subtleties, especially as a late-stage move unfolds. A stock may not be down 15 or 20 percent on large volume. Maybe it's down only 4 or 5 percent, but the volume is the largest since the beginning of a big move. If other violations have occurred, it's definitely a major warning.

DryShips Inc. (DRYS) flashed several warnings as it entered the final stages of its advance just before the stock topped out and lost 99 percent of its value (Figure 9-11). The stock ran up 8 out of 11 days and then another 6 out of 8 days, with one of those days being the largest up day since the beginning of the move. Then a key reversal occurred on the heaviest volume since the beginning of the stock's big move. The final sell signal came on October 30, 2007, when the stock experienced its largest decline on overwhelming volume. Lumber Liquidators followed a similar pattern (Figure 9-12).

Figure 9-11   DryShips (DRYS) 2007. Stock displayed a plethora of classic signals. The stock subsequently declined by 99.8 percent.

Figure 9-12   Lumber Liquidators (LL) 2013–2014. Stock topped in November 2013. It attempted to emerge from a faulty, late-stage base. Five trading days later, the stock experienced the largest drop on heavy volume.

THE BREAKEVEN OR BETTER RULE

As you look at scenarios for selling, consider the use of a trailing stop and, specifically, following the "breakeven or better" rule. The rule is predicated on the 50-day moving average, an intermediate-term trend-line that plays an important role in many key leaders. Let's assume that Stock XYZ is coming out of a base and you purchase it at $50 a share. You set an 8 percent stop at $46. The stock moves higher, never touch-ing your stop, until it's up 5, 10, or maybe 15 percent. While the stock is advancing, the 50-day moving average will eventually start moving higher. As the uptrend continues, the 50-day moving average will reach your breakeven point of $50 a share. Now it's time to switch your stop placement to the 50-day moving average (Figure 9-13). I like to wait for a close below it, and sometimes I try to give it until Friday to see how the stock closes the week. As the 50-day line moves up and catches up to your breakeven price, the 50-day moving average is now your stop. The 50-day line becomes a trailing stop to protect your profits. This is why we call the rule breakeven or better.

Figure 9-13   Medivation (MDVN) 2011–2012.

In the later stages of the bull market, you will want to sell into strength and nail down quick profits when you have them. However, this rule can be especially helpful in the beginning of a new bull market as stocks start to make their advance, and a trailing stop can help keep you in for much of a big move. Some leaders can go an amazing distance before they close below the 50-day line.

THE FREE ROLL

Once a stock moves up two or three times your stop (a 2R or 3R trade), it gives you a lot of flexibility. There are a couple of things you can do. Let's say you set a 7 percent stop on your new buy, and the stock moves up 14 percent over the next week or two. Your first option is to sell half and move your stop to breakeven. You are now free rolling the back half—the worst you can do is break even on the remaining shares—and guarantee yourself a 7 percent profit.

The second option is to sell half and maintain your original 7 percent stop; again, you are free rolling the trade. The worst you can do is break even on the entire position, while giving the stock enough room to fluctuate above your 7 percent stop. You are financing the risk on the back half with the profit you took on the front half. Of course, you can always just hold and risk it all, but I love to hear the cash register ring. And I'm always trying to get myself into a position where I can "free roll" for a larger gain.

THE BACK STOP

When you enter a trade, your initial stop is at a predetermined loss—for example, a 10 percent stop (e.g., you buy a stock at $20 and set the stop 10 percent below, at $18). As the stock advances and you attain a decent profit, the next logical level to protect is your entry price or breakeven point. The third is a profit protection stop, which, as the name implies, stops you out of the trade with a gain. I call this a back stop. Although it gives the stock some room to fluctuate, it draws a line in the sand that I'm not willing to let the stock fall below.

A back stop is not a trailing stop; it doesn't move up in lockstep with the price. The back stop is different, because rather than moving in increments with the advancing price, you are setting the level based on the amount of profit you want to protect, and then allowing the stock to fluctuate above that level. This could help you stay with a trade and not choke it off too soon. As the stock price moves up, you can then move up your back stop and draw a new line in the sand, protecting an even greater profit.

I often will set my back stop at or above my average gain, because I want to maintain my average, at least, and preferably improve on it over time. Once again, you need to know the truth about your trading and understand your personal math. Let's say your average gain is 10 percent. The stock you're holding is up 20 percent. You could move your stop and back stop the 10 percent level to hold for a bigger profit, or you could sell half and back stop the rest. There are numerous variations to experiment with.

Here's another scenario: Your stock is up 15 percent, a percentage that you're pretty happy with; if the stock were to rally more, say 20 percent, you would very likely sell. But the next morning, the stock unexpectedly gaps even higher than that; now you're up 23 percent. Setting a back stop at 20 percent locks in your original profit target, while allowing you to see if there is any follow-through on the gap up. In situations like this, I've had stocks go on to make much larger moves, which I could capture by setting my back stop at a level that I was content with. I have done this with a stop at 5 or 10 cents or even a dollar or two and enjoyed much bigger profits because the stock never came down to hit my back stop.

You Will Always Sell Too Soon or Too Late

The goal of stock trading is to make a decent profit on your investments—not to try to be right all the time. It's not about getting the low and the high either, which is nearly impossible to do even occasionally, let alone consistently. Bottom line: if you don't sell early, you're going to sell late.

Ninety-nine percent of the time it will be one or the other. If you held onto a stock that you bought at $20 and saw it rise to $40, and it then fell from $40 to $30, you'd probably kick yourself for not selling sooner. However, one the most demoralizing experiences is to watch a stock you own skyrocket and then tumble, taking back all your profit, or worse still turning into a loss. Remember, your goal is to make more on your winners than you lose on your losers, and to nail down good-size profits when you have them.

You might as well know something right up front: you're almost never going to get the highest price, but it's not necessary to do so to achieve superperformance. Instead of worrying about selling at the high or buying at the low, concern yourself with what trading is about: making a good-size profit and repeating it over and over. The goal is to sell stocks higher than you buy them. This has little to do with where the stock trades relative to where it once traded.

EARLY STAGE EXCEPTION

After the stock breaks out of a base, you are looking for tennis ball action (see Section 1) from natural reactions to determine if you should hold longer. If the price action is strong and the stock is resilient, give it a chance to make a larger move. After the stock goes through several pullbacks and then returns to new high ground, it's time to start looking for signs that the price is getting too far ahead of itself—particularly if the stock is moving up from a late-stage base. If you're a swing trader, you might not require a late-stage base to consider selling.

Included in the Section 1 discussion was David Ryan's MVP indicator; when 12 of 15 days up signaled breakout strength that suggests you should hold for a larger move. It may sound confusing that now I'm telling you essentially the opposite: to sell when you have 70 percent more up days than down days. That's because now we're talking about a late-stage exhaustion move versus an early-stage breakout move.

As with any set of rules, there are exceptions. In this case, there is a significant caveat if the type of action described above occurs from an *early stage base* after the first run-up following a market correction (Figure 9-14). In this scenario, these actions are a bullish signal. And that's why you need to know where you are in the stock's cycle. What looks like exhaustion in buying activity in the late stage, giving you rationale to sell a stock, is actually a bullish sign early on and would compel you to keep holding on. Know where the stock is in its life cycle and respond accordingly (Figures 9-15 and 9-16).

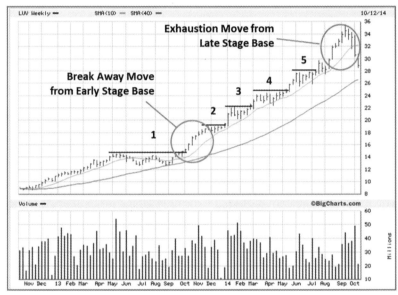

Figure 9-14   Southwest Airlines (LUV) 2013–2014. +127% in 11 months.

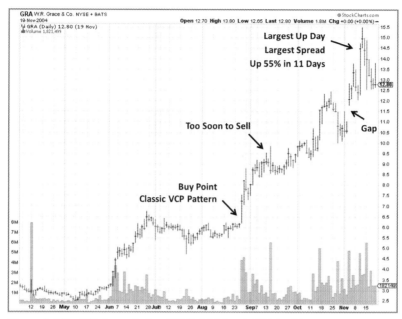

Figure 9-15   WR Grace & Co. (GRA) 2004. +147% in 55 days.

Figure 9-16   Amgen (AMGN) 1990. +360% in 26 months.

Know When—and Why—to Sell

While much of your focus, particularly as you start trading, will naturally be on honing your buying criteria, don't neglect to pay attention to where, how, and why to sell. Just as with your buying setup, your selling also requires rules, whether you sell into strength or weakness. Having rules about sell signals that trigger when and where to sell, you will be making decisions based on solid rationale, instead of giving into your emotions—particularly fear and regret.

EIGHT KEYS TO UNLOCKING SUPERPERFORMANCE

There is an old saying: "You can't have your cake and eat it, too"—conventional wisdom meant to dampen people's expectations of what is and is not possible in life. But this attitude does not apply to my trading, where a corollary to the "cake" axiom is you can't capture big returns unless you also take big risk. This simply is not true.

To dispel this old, limited thinking, I offer my Eight Keys to Unlocking Superperformance—and to do so with low risk. The Four Keys to Generating Big Performance address the upside, while the Four Keys to Limiting Drawdowns protect your two most precious assets as a trader: your capital and your confidence. Together, they form the nucleus of what you need to do to achieve outstanding performance. **If you want big returns in the stock market, you have to learn how to accomplish two things: 1. Make big money when you're correct, and 2. Avoid big drawdowns when you're wrong.** In this section, I'm going to show you how. One caveat: Be prepared to have your assumptions challenged and your thinking flipped 180 degrees. This guidance is not the conventional wisdom. In fact, it contradicts most of the advice you would get from many of the so-called "experts."

THE FOUR KEYS TO GENERATING BIG PERFORMANCE

KEY 1: TIMING

Top of the list of what most "experts" say you *can't* do in trading is time the market. Yes, you can time the market. I've been doing it successfully for decades. Simply stated, timing is everything—in life and in trading. We often hear how someone got a lucky break by being at the right place at the right time. For example, Harrison Ford was cast as Hans Solo in the *Star Wars* movies after he was asked to step in to read a part while working as a carpenter on the set. An incredible break, but one for which the actor had prepared for years.

Achieving lasting success is not like winning the lottery—a few "lucky" numbers and voila! Many years of hard work are required to prepare for those "right time, right place" moments, so that when they occur you are truly equipped to seize the opportunities. The same applies to trading. You can't wake up one morning, throw a dart at a board, pick a stock, and expect to make money consistently. Trading at a high level is about finding those "right time, right place" moments in the market for which you have properly prepared.

As for those who say "you can't time the market," that usually means *they* can't time the market, so they can't imagine anyone being able to do so. Keep in mind, your timing isn't always going to be correct. In fact, you are likely to be correct only about half the time. It's how you manage the winners and the losers that will turn your timing into performance. **If you ever want to do anything great with your life, you must stop believing those who say you can't. This naysaying always comes from the mouths of people who never did it themselves.** Instead, start believing those who say you can, those successful individuals who have been to the mountaintop already and experienced the vistas.

In the pursuit of superperformance, timing separates the big performers from the mediocre. To generate big returns, you must compound your money rapidly. The faster you can generate profits, the bigger your results are going to be (e.g., 10 percent per month instead of 20 percent a year). The precision required to get into and out of positions at the most opportune points means timing your buys and sells.

When you are trading individual stocks, especially smaller, under-followed names, timing becomes much easier than trying to figure out the direction of the entire market day to day. Your job is to time your purchases along the "line of least resistance." As discussed previously, the line of least resistance is the price level from which a stock can move very quickly, making a large-scale advance in a short period of time. I call these velocity trades.

As a trader pursuing superperformance, you should always be on the lookout for velocity trades, which can make gains on the order of 20, 30, or 50 percent over a few weeks or a few months. With velocity trades, you can compound your money very rapidly. Even with a 20 or 30 percent return made over a few weeks or a few months, you can compound your money with several trades over a longer period and amass a significant total return.

To time the market, or even one stock, you need to utilize some kind of formalized approach with rules that improve your chances of capturing above-market gains. Charts are essential. My approach utilizes a chart blueprint known as the volatility contraction pattern (VCP), which has become extremely popular among attendees of my seminars and readers of my first book. (For a review of VCP and how I use charts to time my buys, you can turn to Sections 6 and 7).

Key 2: Don't Diversify

If you have a significant edge, diversification doesn't help you; it dilutes you. Bottom line: you are not going to achieve big returns consistently if you are widely diversified. To generate a big return consistently, you need to be concentrated among the very best names—somewhere between four and twelve, depending on your account size and risk tolerance. In fact, when things work well, I like to have most of my money in the top four or five names that I am following closely. Regardless of what you may have heard or read, there is no need for an individual investor to be widely diversified.

My argument for concentration flies in the face of conventional wisdom, which states that diversification is the best way to protect yourself against risk and still reap a decent return. First of all, I'm not interested in a "decent" return; I want a huge return. And second, I want to be able to control my risk. Those who favor diversification argue that if one stock (or sector) goes down, another one will go up, and it will even out your exposure and smooth out your volatility. But by spreading your buys across market sectors and among many different stocks, you will end up with an average. If you're lucky, your return will mirror the best-performing market index (in which case you would probably be better off just buying the S&P 500 ETF SPY for broad market exposure). Of course, you might get lucky by being diversified during an incredible bull market and produce a strong return because the entire market is going up. But diversification won't do that for you consistently, year in and year out. For that, you need to be concentrated in the very best names at the right time.

If you want to pursue superperformance—regularly producing annual returns of 40 to 100 percent or more—you will need to convincingly beat the market. In other words, you must produce "alpha." To be clear, being concentrated doesn't mean putting all your money in one stock. Do that, and you could wake up one morning and discover half or all your money is gone! You can achieve superperformance with a concentration among a handful of names. Consider the example of Ken Heebner of Capital Growth Management. Ken manages billions with a relatively concentrated portfolio, rarely ever going above 15 to 20 names for 80 percent of his capital. If Ken can manage billions of dollars in just 20 names, surely you can manage with 5 or 10.

I'm not suggesting you load up on stocks and trade aggressively all the time; just the opposite. **The way to make big money in stocks is to be concentrated at the right time—when things are working and moving in your direction—and to trade lightly when trading gets difficult.** That means you must stay on top of your stocks. You can't possibly do that effectively if you own dozens of names. With a concentrated portfolio, you can keep a close eye on every name and move quickly into or out of positions. You can increase your market exposure on a moment's notice, and you can go to cash just as rapidly. Speed is your big advantage.

The other reason why I dislike diversification is that it gives a false sense of security, as if you can buy a bunch of names and then forget about them. This is the exact opposite of the thinking you must adopt to achieve superperformance. By concentrating your portfolio—and your attention—to a handful of carefully selected and closely watched names, you can consistently generate a meaningful return. You will be able to make big money when you're right.

If you think being concentrated is risky, I offer the example of my own personal performance, which came with little drawdown right up to this day. In 2003, a large money management firm approached me about consulting for it. When the firm asked to audit my account, I said absolutely. A small team of its accountants went over my statements and trade confirmations; they even spoke to the brokerage firm where I placed my trades. When the results came back, the head of the money management firm called me. "We can't figure out how you're doing this," he said, "but you have an alpha (excess return above the market) of 212 percent and a beta (volatility) of 0.43." During this period, 88 percent of my months were positive with only one down quarter. It was the most incredible performance they had ever seen, all done with little drawdown or risk.

I told them that I was producing those returns by doing things that most institutions would never allow me to do because they would consider it too risky. But as I explained, it was just the opposite. Being concentrated kept me focused in the very best names and forced me to keep super tight risk control.

KEY 3: TURNOVER IS NOT TABOO!
Another rule among most money managers and mutual funds is to keep portfolio turnover low because of commissions and for tax reasons. Buying and selling frequently is frowned upon for them. But if you have an edge and you're running a concentrated portfolio, turnover can be a good thing. Trading in and out of positions could further your goal of compounding your money rapidly, if you have an edge. With every trade,

you are trying to make as much as possible in the shortest possible time frame, so you can go on to the next potential winning trade and maximize compounding. That's not to say you shouldn't hold a stock if it continues to act well, but you want to lose as little time value as possible.

Here's a simplified example: Let's say that you're flipping a coin, and every time it comes up heads you make $2, and when it comes up tails you lose $1. Given the statistical probability of heads being the result half the time and a 2:1 payoff, the more you flip, the more you make because of the mathematical edge. An edge in the stock market works much the same way. I'm not going to keep myself from selling one stock and buying another because I'm concerned about having a high turnover rate or because I will have to pay taxes on the gain; my goal is to have gains to pay taxes on. I buy a stock when the probability is high for reward versus risk, and I sell when the risk of owning it gets too high. I never make a sell decision based on turnover or tax reasons.

When I first started trading more than 30 years ago, I had to control my turnover because commissions were very costly (about $350 per round trip). It took a while to cover the cost of the commissions before there was any profit to be had, especially because my account was small. Today, there is no reason to limit turnover, even for a very small trading account. Commissions are inexpensive, and you have the ease of clicking on a button (even from your phone or tablet) to execute a trade. As stocks move freely up and down, there are many opportunities to buy and sell swings.

Bottom line: if you get a sell signal, get out. Or, if something looks more appealing, move out of a less attractive name and into something better. Traders don't get married to a stock—they just "date." **Your money should always be moving to where you are going to reap the best performance, and moving out of troubled situations that put your capital at risk.** You may even move to cash when there are few compelling stocks. As a result, much of your turnover will be the result of cutting losses and managing risk. You want to hold a key leader for a big move when the time is right, but don't underestimate the power of smaller wins compounded. With an edge, turnover is good.

Key 4: Always Maintain the
Risk/Reward Relationship

Here, all the keys to generating superperformance come together: timing, a concentrated portfolio, the willingness to move into and out of positions, and now, managing risk versus reward. You are poised to take advantage of a huge upside, with protection that allows you to move out of a position quickly, if and when something moves against you. By continuously rebalancing the risk and reward, you negate or mitigate any downside to being highly concentrated among a few names in your portfolio. **You should take a short-term approach to losses and a relatively longer-term approach to gains; that means you cut your losses and let your winners run.** Regardless of the time frame, I always maintain the risk/reward relationship. For example, if I think there's a decent chance that a stock can trade up 15 percent, I set my stop at 7 or 8 percent or less. Even if it's a 50/50 chance that I'm right, it's a good risk/reward play because I'm only risking 7 percent to gain 15 percent.

You should evaluate your position every day on the basis of risk versus reward. Consider the following example: Back in December 2010, I bought Body Central (BODY) as it emerged from its first VCP after it went public in October (Figure 10-1). I went into the trade risking 5 per-

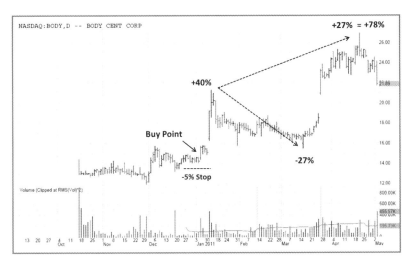

Figure 10-1   Body Central (BODY) 2011.

Chart courtesy of Interactive Data

cent. The stock shot up 40 percent in just six days. I sold into the strength and nailed down a great short-term profit.

Now, let's assume I moved my stop to breakeven and held the stock—for a larger profit—and three-months later I was able to get out right near the high when the stock showed me a 78 percent gain. Would that have been a good trade? No. Why? Because the goal is to always maintain the risk/reward relationship. To realize that 78 percent gain I would have to let the stock drop 27 percent to gain 27 percent more. That's a 1:1 reward/risk ratio.

The Four Keys to Limiting Drawdowns

Now that you've addressed the upside, it's time to consider the downside. Even with precise timing and a concentrated portfolio among stocks that you're watching closely, you won't achieve superperformance if your hard-earned profits get eaten up by large drawdowns. You can have a 50 percent return two years in a row, and then suffer a 50 percent drawdown the third year, and end up with virtually no progress. Consider the math:

$$100 + (50\% \ gain) = 150 + (50\% \ gain) =$$
$$225 - (50\% \ loss) = 112.50 \ (4\% \ per \ annum)$$

Avoiding large drawdowns requires a change in thinking. Don't accept the conventional wisdom that "you can't have big profits without taking big risks." If you think this way, you will come to accept and even expect large drawdowns, which you can, in fact, keep to a minimum.

Every technical stock trader talks about setting stops to reduce risk by limiting losses to a predetermined level. **While stops are a great discipline, you must set them at a level that makes sense so that you are controlling risk in relation to reward. If you don't maintain the correct balance, you might find yourself taking on big risk in return for only a small payoff.** The objective here is to do the opposite: take a small risk in return for a big potential reward.

You are not running a massive, market-moving portfolio like a big mutual fund manager. No matter how "big" you think you are, as an individual investor your buys and sells are not going to move the market, even in most thinly traded, illiquid stocks. This is a tremendous advantage, allowing you to manage the risk/reward relationship very effectively. Liquidity facilitates speed and the freedom to move in and out or jockey for position. This next set of keys will help you lower portfolio volatility and limit your drawdowns.

KEY 1: SELL INTO STRENGTH

Always keep in mind, it's generally better to sell early than late. A stock you bought has risen steadily; your position is up 20, 30, or 40 percent. . . . So what do you do? The answer divides the pros from the amateurs.

Professional traders sell into strength. They want to sell when there are eager buyers. Amateurs, on the other hand, get happy and giddy, thinking that their rising stock is never going down. Then greed sets in and they don't sell. Even when a 30 percent gain turns into a 40 or 50 percent gain, they refuse to get out while the getting is good.

Granted, after you sell, the stock may keep on going, rallying even further without you in it. You can grumble and complain about money you didn't make because you got out after, say, a 40 percent gain and the stock ended up doubling or tripling over a longer period of time. That's going to happen.

But if you fail to sell into strength, you'll set yourself up for a far bigger problem than potential profits left on the table. If you wait too long to sell, the uptrend will end and the stock will come crashing back down. You might shake off the first dip—after all, stocks rarely rise or fall in one direction. But then a 5 percent drop turns into a 15 percent drop, and now you really don't want to sell because you're kicking yourself for not selling higher. Wait too long, though, and the stock could break even harder, giving back all or most of your gains. When you do sell, your profit is either greatly reduced or fully negated, and all because you were afraid of missing out on more upside.

It's far better to sell into strength than wait too long and lose all or most of the sizeable gain you once had. **When you sell into strength, your equity value is at its highest point. If you want to maintain an**

**equity curve that consistently stair-steps up, you should learn how to
sell when you have a decent gain while the stock is advancing.**

Waiting too long to sell also runs the risk of losing time value. When
you hold a stock through a significant correction, you may have to go
through weeks, months, or longer before it starts another leg up. During
that time, you're tying up your money instead of getting out at a profit and
moving on to the next best opportunity.

Remember the lesson on time value: thanks to the power of compounding, if you can get a small but consistent return and repeat it over
and over, it could be far more productive than trying for a bigger return
that takes several months or even years to produce.

Time Value and the Power of Compounding

> *Two 40 percent returns = 96 percent return*
> *Four 20 percent returns = 107 percent return*
> *Twelve 10 percent returns = 214 percent return*

These numbers are eye-opening for many novice traders who think
that their only hope of achieving superperformance is finding that one
"moonshot" stock. But eight trades that produce a 10 percent profit will
more than double your money. And 12 trades (one per month on average) that produce a 10 percent return will more than triple your money.
So ask yourself: how much easier would it be to find a dozen stocks that
go up 10 percent, versus finding three or four that produce a 40 percent
return, or one that doubles or triples? This is opportunity cost at work.

KEY 2: TRADE SMALL BEFORE YOU TRADE BIG

When you're "right"—when your analysis is working and your timing is
on target—you can trade larger size per trade and increase your overall
exposure. You can get more aggressive because what you're doing is prov-
ing effective in the market and you've built a cushion. The key here is you
build on success.

But when things aren't working so well—perhaps your analysis is correct, but your timing is off—you can't remain aggressive. That's when it's

time to slow down or even take a break from trading as you analyze why you're out of sync with the market. This is the essence of letting the market guide you, instead of following your opinions or hunches. Developing this self-control will train you to listen to and trust the market, not your "gut." Your intuition has no business in your trading. Personal feelings are seldom a substitute for facts.

Here's how it works in real-life trading: You make a few purchases from your list of stocks that you're watching as they trigger buy points. Once you've logged a few gains or a number of your positions are showing some net progress, these results will "finance" the risk for bigger trades. Let's say you make $1,000 on one trade and then $1,000 on another, for a total of $2,000. You can now afford to trade a little larger. You can risk $2,000 to make $4,000, because that risk is already "financed" by the $2,000 in banked profits. Moreover, you're trading more aggressively on the heels of profitable trades, pyramiding your way to bigger positions, instead of working your way out of a hole.

When losses mount, it takes a toll not only financially, but also emotionally. Your confidence gets shaken. But by following the market's guidance as it "tells" you whether your strategy and timing are on or off, you won't ever get too far off track. As a result, your capital and your confidence will remain intact.

Losses are valuable information that things aren't working. Your timing is off, or perhaps the market is weighing on stocks in general. Why would you want to throw good money after bad if something isn't working well? If you do, then your ego is more invested in your opinion than in the actual market. This rule is one of the most important disciplines to keep your drawdowns low. Yet, most investors don't operate this way. When things get difficult and losses mount, most investors "revenge trade" and try to get it back quickly. This means trading larger or doubling up on losing positions to get back the money they lost. Occasionally and in the short run, this can work and bail you out of a losing streak. Over the long run, though, it will only lead to large drawdowns and invite disaster.

The Three Deadly Trader Traps

1.   Emotions. Causing you to do things that are irrational
2.   Opinions. Forming an idea that limits your vision
3.   Ego. Keeping you from admitting and correcting mistakes

KEY 3: ALWAYS TRADE DIRECTIONALLY

This is especially important if you control risk with the use of relatively tight stops: You must trade directionally. If you try to go against the trend, you will seldom be correct. Once a trend is established—for example, a stock you like has come under selling pressure—it's very risky to buy, thinking that at some point it will come back. There is usually a low likelihood of that stock reversing the trend and making a *sustained* move in your direction precisely when you expect. If you're using relatively tight stops, even a small decline could stop you out and produce a losing trade. These losses can add up, so the goal is to buy at exactly the precise moment when the risk of loss is minimal.

Once again, this is a case of letting the market, and not your own opinions, dictate what you should do. When you buy, do so in the direction of the trade. If a stock you like has come down in price, wait until it starts to turn around again before you commit your hard-earned capital.

I never buy a falling stock. I always trade directionally. This applies to all time frames, from long-term investing to swing trading and even day trading. Allowing the market to guide you puts you in sync with it, which increases your chances of making a profit and limiting losses. Over time you will, at a minimum, experience smaller drawdowns.

KEY 4: PROTECT YOUR BREAKEVEN POINT
ONCE YOU'VE ATTAINED A DECENT GAIN

This key requires a little more finesse than the typical hard-and-fast rule, but it starts with understanding the premise: protect your principal as soon as possible. How and when this occurs will depend a lot on market conditions and how well your trading is progressing. If market conditions are challenging, I will be quicker to protect the downside, moving my stop up more quickly and being less forgiving of any adverse moves against me. If my strategy and timing are in sync with the market, then I will be more forgiving and allow my stocks a bit more room. **As your trade becomes profitable and shows a decent gain, you want to protect your breakeven point or at least move up your stop to lessen your risk.**

When you enter a trade, your stop is set below the entry point at a predetermined loss. But as the trade becomes increasingly profitable, you don't want to keep the stop at that level. To protect your breakeven, you need to move it up to the price you paid. It's important that you hold off on raising your stop until the price moves up a decent amount, otherwise you won't allow enough room for normal fluctuation and you'll choke off the trade.

The Eight Keys in Your Hands

The Eight Keys to Unlocking Superperformance—and all the rules presented in this book—are the culmination of the lessons I have learned, which changed my performance from mediocre to stellar. I realized that to get big returns I didn't necessarily need to find giant winners in the stock market (although that remains my ultimate goal). But while I'm looking for those stocks that make huge moves, I can still pursue a very strong performance with smaller, solid gains that compound my money. This "Plan B" allows me to turn 15 to 20 percent winners into triple-digit annual returns, instead of waiting for that one big stock that may or may not show up this year.

When I started trading for a living, I had to find a way to extract consistent profits from the market. I learned that smaller moves can compound into sizable gains with intelligent market timing, a concentrated portfolio, and some turnover because you're nailing down profits by selling into strength and moving on to the next opportunity. Trading in this way takes care of your upside, with a solid cumulative return. You also protect the downside to keep the profits you make by limiting losses, while letting your winners finance your risk.

Big rewards with small risks are possible. It is the best of both worlds—truly "having your cake and eating it, too." Don't let anyone tell you otherwise. It requires discipline, but you can do it, because I did and still do today.

THE CHAMPION TRADER MINDSET

Mark Minervini with Performance Coach Jairek Robbins

Jairek Robbins is a friend of mine for whom I have a great deal of respect. And although he has a loyal following and is internationally recognized as a successful motivational speaker, I consider him a relatively undiscovered gem. As a personal performance coach, Jairek specializes in helping individuals and organizations accelerate their results and live a better life with more purpose and effectiveness. And as a student of human behavior, he understands the negative emotions that lead to self-sabotage and impede performance. Jairek is the author of the best-selling book *Live It*. He's an expert in neuro-linguistic programming (NLP), a very powerful technology that has made a huge difference not only in my trading, but my entire life.

As part of my preparation for the 2016 Master Trader Program workshop, I sat down with Jairek to discuss the emotional pitfalls and psychological triggers that make superperformance difficult for most to achieve, and what traders can do to overcome them. Our conversation specifically addressed cognitive conditioning and NLP techniques that could help individuals improve their performance, lower their stress, and enjoy a better quality of life as a stock trader. Our conversation was so powerful, I felt compelled to include it in this book.

Mark Minervini: Over the years, I've come to realize that fear is the number one emotion that causes traders to sabotage their discipline. Fear of missing out causes them to chase stocks and buy past the point at which they know they should. Fear of loss causes them to sell too soon and take small profits in stocks that show no real reason for concern. And fear of making a mistake keeps traders from being able to pull the trigger decisively. How can investors deal with their fears so they can trade more effectively?

Jairek Robbins: There is an emotional state called detachment that allows you to operate at your absolute best. With detachment from the outcome, you have the ability to access a strategy with total certainty. You know that sometimes you'll win and sometimes you'll lose. You detach from what happens once you place the trade. Detachment, which is grounded in eastern philosophy, keeps you from being affected by negative emotions such as fear. To achieve that state, you have to create what I call your "emotional forcefield." To do that, you have to "fill up and fuel up daily."

Here's an analogy—it's going to sound silly, but bear with me: Imagine you're a can of soda. If you are only half full, even a child could crush the sides of the can. But if you were filled and pressure-sealed with positive pressure pushing outward, you couldn't be dented even by a strong adult. A full and sealed soda can is impossible to dent. Traders need to do that for themselves, every day. They do that by creating routines for themselves as they prepare for the trading day—what will fill up, fuel up, and pressurize themselves before they even step into the space where they trade.

One example—and Mark, I know you practice this one every day—is the "mental rehearsal." It's what Muhammad Ali used to prepare for every match, and what other major athletes rely on. Before going on to explain, let me point out one important distinction. A mental rehearsal is *not* visualization—and that's where a lot of people go wrong. Positive visualization is imagining the best possible results. But that's not reality! For a trader, that would mean visualizing every trade going your way, which is impossible. If you visualize everything positive and you have a loss, your nervous system freaks out, and all your fears come true.

Mastering those fears requires a mental rehearsal. In your mind, you start out with the mental picture of what you want to see to make a great trade. By following your plan, step by step, you move into and out of the market effortlessly. However, you also picture yourself doing the exact same thing—diligently following your plan and identifying the perfect setup—but this time you envision the market going against you. The stock doesn't follow through the way you had expected. Your trade is stopped out at a small loss. You see yourself accepting that loss, taking a breath, shaking it off, and sitting back down to identify your next trade. Your mental rehearsal includes seeing yourself achieving positive outcomes on some trades, and getting hit by obstacles and having losses on others. The more you rehearse and see yourself able to stick to your discipline and your plan, no matter the outcome, the better you'll be able to tame your anxiety. You will see yourself resisting the temptation to chase a stock. You see yourself holding your stops and getting out of a trade with a small loss, even if the stock turns around and rallies without you on board. You know these things are going to happen to you, just like they do to every trader.

Developing the ability to mentally rehearse these scenarios *every day, before you trade* will prepare you for whatever comes at you—just like Muhammad Ali prepared himself to take a punch and feel the pain, and continue fighting. When that punch landed for real in the ring, he had a mental edge that kept him fighting and made him the best.

Mark: That's a fantastic explanation with some very practical advice. Here's how I like to explain it. You have to go from outcome to process. Using another sports analogy, if you're up at bat, you are not going to hit home runs by being focused or preoccupied with the scoreboard. Your goal is to score runs. But if you put all your attention on the task at hand, you will hit well, and the score will reflect it. My own personal performance went from mediocre to stellar when I finally said to heck with the money. I'm taking my focus off the scoreboard. I'm going to focus on being the best trader I can be and concentrate on making every decision a quality choice. Then the results appeared. Making money is the result or by-product of effectively carrying out a well-thought-out plan. Focusing on the money or the outcome will only distract you from the work you need to do to achieve the desired result. The money will only come after you execute your plan. So, that's what I focus on.

So, Jairek, here's another question. To prepare for the trading day—mind and body—what can traders do to optimize their efforts?

Jairek: As part of your daily preparation, you want to activate your body and optimize your mental and emotional state. In addition to the mental rehearsal, you need to get your body physically active. A great tool is a small trampoline, called a rebounder, which is one of the most effective ways of engaging your body. Diaphragmatic breathing (in which you breathe deeply using your diaphragm, versus shallow breathing) brings you alive. This type of deep breathing moves three to four times the lymph in your body as normal breathing.

Here is a technique I learned from an ex–Navy Seal—it's called "box breathing." You breathe in through your nose for four seconds, hold your breath for four seconds; then you breathe out through your mouth for four seconds and hold like that for four seconds. Do this for five minutes. This allows you to focus your mind by concentrating on your breath. Five minutes of box breathing disassociates you from anything else. If you are completely focused on your breathing, your mind cannot form fears or anxieties or negative thoughts. And, breathing like this gets oxygen to your brain. (A lot of people stop breathing when they get fearful.) You are recentered emotionally and refueled with oxygen!

Mark: That's so true. I used to tell traders who worked for me that I could close my eyes and know how their trading was going simply by listening to their breathing. If I started hearing labored breathing, I knew the pressure was on. I know the importance of proper breathing. My wife practices Reiki and does daily breathing exercises. Breathing with intentionality can really help your focus, train you to be in control of your anxiety, and improve the way you function under stress.

By the way, I just bought my first rebounder, and I love it! To keep me energized, I hit tennis balls during the day and have a sit-up bench right outside my office; I do this during lulls in trading. The rebounder just added another way to keep my blood flowing; I'm keeping it right near my office.

Jairek, you've discussed the emotional and physical preparation, what else can help traders prepare mentally for the trading day—especially to master their fear? As I've found in all my years of teaching and coaching traders, and now with my seminars, if I give people rules, that's not enough. For one thing, they don't always follow the rules. Trading is not a game of certainty, but a game of probability—and the rules are what move the odds in their favor. I can teach them my strategy and the mechanics, but they go home with their idiosyncrasies. And so they lose their confidence, and in some cases regress into a myopic state focusing on the most recent trades and losing perspective or what I call a reference to the whole.

Jairek: Here's another preparation that can help affirm discipline and adherence to the rules. Every day, before you trade, review what happened the day before. First, you identify what great things happened the day before in your trading—not just the wins, but also when you stuck to your discipline, like getting stopped out for a small loss. Second, identify two or three lessons learned that led to good results—or that you realize now from painful outcomes. Write down the lessons learned every day. Some traders will find, as they write down the lessons from the day before, that they keep repeating the same ones, over and over. That will keep occurring until they master whatever it is they need to learn. Third, ask yourself, "How am I going to improve today?" Again, write it down so you can record where you see the need for improvement.

Starting the trading day with these three questions—what went great, what were the lessons learned, and how am I going to improve—will help traders learn from their results and improve. Bringing it all together—mental rehearsal, box breathing, activating your body, and asking these three questions—you can become better prepared for the trading day. Preparation also helps you come from a place of abundance, which is not about money, but about all those things in your life that money can't buy: relationships, health, eyesight, hearing . . . All these things equip you abundantly for the challenge of trading. When you come from a place of mental and emotional abundance, you will trade better.

Mark: Yes! It's all about empowering yourself. To do that you need to understand yourself. Each trader is different. For some, buying correctly is the problem, while for someone else selling may be the issue. I always recommend that you print out charts of your trades and mark with a pen where you bought and sold. As you study these trades, you will almost always find a common denominator, something that you do repeatedly.

Jairek, you are an expert in NLP, or how language is processed in the brain. Twenty-five years ago, I first learned about NLP and have incorporated it into my trading and in my life. I have read countless books on NLP and continue to practice it to this day. It has been a very effective tool for me personally. What types of NLP techniques do you recommend to help traders improve how they manage their life and their trading?

Jairek: NLP is used in cognitive behavioral coaching, which we can think of as a mix of your behavior and your thoughts and emotions. The objective is to train yourself to fall into the right patterns. A Duke University study, for example, found that more than 40 percent of the patterns of what we do every day are nothing more than habits and routines! Applying that to trading, that means 40 percent of what you do is not cognitive—it's not a thought that you've decided to have and act on. Rather, it's predecided and built into your nervous system as a habit.

Ask yourself: What habits have I built into my trading already? Which are helping and which are hurting me? Charles Duhigg's book *The Power of Habit* shows that every habit has only three parts: a cue (or trigger), a routine, and a reward. Starting with identifying the negative patterns in your trading—what you repeat continuously that is hurting your ability to trade. Maybe it's how a certain scenario in your trading triggers your fears, which causes you to act in a certain way. That's not you experiencing fear—it's you *doing* fear!

Mark: Yes, I love Charles's book. I explain to people that trading is a unique challenge because of what happens when you're wrong. If you apply for a job and they don't hire you, or you write a manuscript and a publisher says, "No, not interested," you may be discouraged, but you can try again. With trading, every time you have a negative outcome it costs you financially. A trader can make a mistake that takes $50,000 out of his trading account! At some point, that trader is not only afraid to try—he can't afford to try! The financial losses compound fear and results in a loss of confidence.

Jairek: Using cognitive behavioral coaching, you focus on the thoughts and scenarios that scare you and that stimulate and create fear. Beyond what the market is doing to you, with greater awareness you see how you are creating scenarios and patterns that freak you out. And here's the thing: you get some kind of reward for it. And that's what you have to figure out. Maybe it's the rush of excitement. Or, maybe you enjoy beating yourself up emotionally when you fail. Or, maybe you "reward" yourself for having a bad day because you get to go home with all these big "war stories" of what happened. As you tell what happened, you feel a rush of love and connection from your spouse, partner, or other loved ones. So you set yourself up for losses in order to keep getting that love and attention.

If in examining your patterns and behaviors, you find something like this, you will be able to change your routine. Instead of being triggered by losses, freaking out, and building up a big "war story," you train a different reaction into your body. First, you think of your rules around losses—using stops, keeping your losses small, and so forth. When you take a small loss in accordance with those rules, you celebrate! Jump out of your chair, do a happy dance, go tell someone you love. You want to emotionally stimulate your body so that you *feel* that taking a small loss is a huge victory.

You are replacing those old patterns of going into fear and anxiety over losses that compound until you are in a tailspin. If you can short-circuit those engrained patterns by identifying the old routines and replacing them with new routines, you will experience different outcomes. Instead of envisioning the worst-case scenario, you cut off the old routine immediately and train yourself to experience a small loss as a huge victory.

Mark: Yes, advertising has told us to reward ourselves when we had a hard day. It gives you a reason to go home and pop open a beer. As the ad says: It's Miller time! I have always said that trading triggers the same neurological impulses as going into the jungle unarmed and having a tiger rush out at you! The same adrenaline rush, the same pressure, elevated heart rate, difficulty thinking clearly, etc. That makes the panic even worse, and often at the exact wrong moment. How can a trader manage such a situation and help minimize the emotional hijacking that takes place under stressful trading scenarios?

Jairek: Once again, it goes back to fueling or "filling up," and staying "pressurized." You want to trade at your best—on a 1-to-10 scale, you want to be at a 9 or 10, emotionally, physically, and mentally. If you are at an 8 or below—you are sleep-deprived, you're not eating right, you aren't emotionally detached—you're compromised! Get yourself back to an emotional, physical, and mental 9 or 10 so that you can withstand the pressures of trading.

Mark: Yes, some people ask how I have survived the stress of trading for more than 30 years. My nutrition, exercise, and mental association training has helped keep me trading relatively stress-free. The key is longevity. If you want to last in this business, it's very important to manage your body and mind so you can operate at peak performance.

As I've found, an important key is the meaning traders assign to what they experience. Losses are inevitable. Even a good trader could lose half the time. If people fall apart with every loss, they will defeat themselves. If the meaning they give themselves is "any loss, even a small loss, is a failure," they are going to feel horrible—even when they stick to their rules and take a small loss. Unless they change the meaning they assign to losses, they will likely quit trading. The problem is ego causes traders to hold losses. They don't want to accept being wrong, so they "dig in." They end up holding onto a losing position until a small loss becomes a large loss. Then sell when they can't take the pain anymore. To change this, how can traders let the pain/pleasure cycle work for them, instead of against them?

Jairek: The pain/pleasure cycle goes back to classical conditioning and the example we've all heard about Pavlov and his dogs. Ivan Pavlov was a Russian physiologist who became known in psychology for his work with dogs, studying the interaction between salivation and the action of the stomach. Pavlov's famous experiment was using external stimuli—the sound of a metronome—every time he gave his dogs food, until the sound alone caused them to salivate. The principle here is the same. As mentioned earlier in our discussion of NLP and cognitive behavioral coaching, you are retraining yourself to celebrate when you follow your rules and take a small loss. What you're doing is activating the pleasure cycle of feeling good in the moment because you kept your losses small, and breaking the cycle of associating losses with pain.

The key is to really celebrate. Dance around. Play your favorite music. Watch your favorite YouTube video for five minutes. Do something that gives you pleasure and makes you feel good in the moment. You can't do this just once. You've got to retrain yourself to have a different reaction so that you reprogram your pain/pleasure cycle. Follow the rules, cut your losses to keep them small, and celebrate. Then repeat—every time. Your body will start associating cutting losses quickly and keeping losses small with feeling amazing.

Mark: Yes, I feel great when I take a small loss. It's the big losses that I try to avoid and have associated pain with. However, when I first started trading, I tried to avoid the big loss by holding and hoping the stock would come back and bail me out. As a result, I achieved precisely what I was trying to avoid! That's why having rules and sticking to them is so important. Yet, of those who develop rules, only a handful stick to them religiously. The same phenomenon occurs in dieting, exercising, and trading. What is the reason so few people can maintain discipline for a length of time? How do you go from undisciplined to disciplined?

Jairek: This is a really interesting area in psychology. If you look at behavioral psychology, we're told that we are nothing more than machines and we have the ability to "program the machine" to behave in a certain way. If you look at cognitive psychology, we are emotional beings and our ability to generate the right emotions determines how we will act. Cognitive behavioral psychology is a blend of both approaches. And humanistic psychology focuses on happiness—specifically, what can get a person to the optimal state of happiness and the healthiest version of themselves. Which one to follow? The truth is, all of them are right, some of the time.

In cognitive psychology, the goal is to feel really emotionally great when you do the right thing such as obeying your rules in trading, as well as the negative consequences when you don't. One way is to contemplate all the positive rewards and benefits that will show up in your life when you follow the rules and stay disciplined. Keep a running list of these rewards and benefits, and add five more positive results every day. In addition, you keep a list of all the negative, painful consequences that result from when you don't follow your rules. You add five more negative results to the list every day. And each day you read both lists aloud, top to bottom, so that you really feel the positive results of when you follow the rules, and the negative consequences when you don't.

In humanistic psychology, the goal is becoming the healthiest, happiest, and most fulfilled version of yourself (this starts with Maslow's hierarchy of needs, to ensure your basic needs are met). With self-awareness you begin to identify what would bring you to your happiest and healthiest state, which supports your ability to adhere to the rules. Are you well fed? Are you emotionally balanced? Are you in a healthy environment? You wouldn't expect an Olympian to perform well if he or she was fed half rations, slept four hours a night, and lived in a mold-infested basement with no heat. Of course not. It's obvious that an Olympian would need the best self-care and supportive environment to perform at his or her best. Why would you look at stock trading as any less demanding than what an Olympian endures, especially in terms of emotional and psychological stress? To do well in trading and follow your rules, you need to be at your physical, emotional, and psychological best.

Mark: With the Internet, social media, and 24-hour news, there's the potential for information overload. I have a strategy that has brought me great success. As a result, I have incredible confidence in what I'm doing, and that helps me stick with it and ignore any outside influences or "voices." How does a new trader develop the trust to follow his or her own rules and ignore outside forces?

Jairek: Personally, I don't watch TV and I limit the news I read. The reason is marketing psychology. The purpose of TV programming is to get you mentally and emotionally addicted to watching them. And if you keep watching, those shows will generate more money from advertising. And those advertisements are meant to make you want to buy what you see. That whole process is geared to get you emotionally and mentally addicted.

Obviously, a trader does need information in order to trade. But I would suggest that there is a better option than letting *everything* in. Avoiding information overload starts with your filters so that you are gathering only the information needed. That puts you in charge of the information sources and timing (YouTube and streaming media give you freedom in your viewing selections). Take what you want and shut out the rest. Identify ahead of time what you are looking for, gather that information, and move on. Don't allow yourself to become inundated and distracted by information that's not useful or, worse yet, by the opinions of others that cause you to override your decision making. You want to be like the shopper who goes to the mall to get exactly what you want. If you need new shoes, you don't go to the bookstore or the home furnishing department. If you are like those other shoppers who have to wander the whole store and look at everything, you have much higher probability of getting distracted and letting other people's "opinions" (i.e., merchandising) influence your decision making. Be discerning when it comes to information and put up filters that keep out the noise and the distractions.

Mark: Most traders cannot stick with a strategy or style for very long. As soon as the strategy runs into trouble (as every strategy will), they give up and change. In the industry, we call this "style drift." As a result, they become a jack-of-all-trades and a master of none. How do you develop trust in and long-term commitment to a strategy or discipline to get you through the tough times so you can eventually master it?

Jairek: In his book *Mastery*, Robert Greene looks at the difference between "mastery" and "dabbling." His findings are very enlightening. Let's say you start something new, you make progress and then more progress, until suddenly you hit a plateau where you aren't making any headway. What happens next? The dabbler, who was having fun in the beginning, gets discouraged the minute something gets difficult. The dabbler changes approach or tries something entirely different. It's fun learning for a while, but when it stops working, the dabbler changes again and tries something else.

The master, however, acts differently. When the first plateau is reached, the person pursuing mastery steps back, realizes that these episodes are part of the learning journey and are to be expected, and then commits to learning more and practicing more. Mastery is gained by using these plateaus as opportunities to hone experience. During these lulls, performance may suffer, but the lessons learned during this time and the self-knowledge and discipline gained will propel the person far beyond that plateau. People using this approach will repeat the process of making progress and honing expertise until they achieve mastery. If you only dabble, switching every time something begins to stall until you've gone through dozens of strategies, you will never stick with one long enough to generate the return you want.

Mark: I think that's one of my strongest qualities; I don't dabble in anything. I practice full emersion. I call it removing the excuse factor. When you go all in and commit, it's a totally different framework than when you just dabble. Dabbling gives you a built-in excuse. Well, I'm not serious about this; if I were, I would probably do better. To be great you must commit. How can people detect their "conflicting beliefs" and reset or recalibrate those beliefs to serve their purposes?

Jairek: A conflicting belief would be something like, "I want to generate superperformance and make millions of dollars, but I never want to put in the time to learn or do the homework." That's like saying, "I want to be in the NBA, but never practice basketball." Wanting the results without ever doing the work is a common conflicting belief. You have to watch what you think and how you act. With people who work hard to pursue their goals, the reality of that pursuit shows up on their calendar. Is that true for you? Are you putting in the hours to achieve your goals? Are you committing the time with 110 percent of the required effort? A person who is truly pursuing mastery will show he or she is putting in those hours of commitment. A person who has a conflicting belief—I want the result but not the hard work—will be easy to spot, like the person who claims to be super healthy but his or her physical body is not congruent with that statement.

With trading, you need to look at your reality. Open your trading account and see how "healthy" you are. Are you making money consistently, with rewards that are higher than the risks (losses) that you're taking? Or are you experiencing huge swings? The conflict may very well be between what you want and what you're willing to do to achieve it.

Another conflicting belief gets at what you say you want and what you believe is possible. Some people say they want to be successful, but deep inside they don't believe it's possible. That conflicting belief will hold them back from realizing what they want to achieve. Author Byron Katie seeks to free people from what made them suffer—such as fear and anxiety. One of her techniques is to ask a series of questions. For example, let's say you realize that while you want to be successful, you don't think it's possible. The first question you ask yourself is: "Is it true?" Is it true that you cannot become successful, even though that is your goal? The answer might be yes, or not really, or I don't know. But until you ask the question, you can't expose the conflicting belief. Let's say you answer is "No, it's not possible." Then comes the second question: "Is it true all the time, everywhere, no matter what?" If you're honest, there is no way you can say yes to that one. Nothing is true all the time, everywhere, no matter what—not even the law of gravity! Now you've opened yourself up to another possibility.

The third question to ask yourself is whether you are the kind of person who believes in limitations. Are you acting as the weakest and most anxiety-filled version of yourself? Or, are you the strongest, most confident, most powerful, and most passionate version of yourself? Usually the goal is to be the latter! The fourth question is to ask what you would be without this set of limiting beliefs. Usually, the answer is that you would be not stressed and not fearful. You'd be relaxed and confident. With these four questions, you can turn it around. You realize that it is possible to make it happen. Anytime you catch yourself having conflicting or limiting beliefs, put them through this series of questions.

Mark: What supports a positive mental attitude or state?

Jairek: It's built every day, based on what you feed your mind, what you choose to focus on, what you say to yourself, and how determined you are. Here's an example: Something happens—you make an error in your trading. The question you ask yourself (what you focus on in that moment) is: "What's wrong with me?" Your brain will start analyzing all the data and inputs to tell you what's "wrong" with you. Pretty soon, you will feel terrible in general and bad about yourself. Similarly, a question such as, "Why am I such an idiot?" will direct your brain to give you answers that make you feel you are an idiot. Instead, what if in response to making a mistake or failing to follow your rules, you asked yourself a different question. What would happen if you asked: "Why do I always find a way to make things work?" That would really change things. You'd see yourself as creative and resilient. If you find yourself getting emotionally hijacked, ask yourself questions that will get you back on track. Instead of, "Why did I do that?" you ask, "How can I improve?" Not only do you avoid wasting time moping with the first question, with the second question you set about to learn and improve.

Mark: Yes, ask powerful questions, you get powerful answers. Ask crappy questions, you get crappy answers. I'm often asked, how do you gain the confidence and conviction to trade large positions?

Jairek: By getting it right on a smaller level. Let's say you could trade by risking only pennies. Once you have perfected your rules and honed your discipline, then increasing your trading from pennies to dollars (or many thousands of dollars) should not change anything—because it's not about the money, it's about the discipline. From pennies to dollars, nothing has changed except the amount of cash. Not deviating from your system allows you to win whether you are playing a small game or a larger one. If you go from trading small positions to larger ones and suddenly your "batting average" worsens (fewer wins and more losses), the reason is not the money, but the fact that you didn't follow your system.

Mark: How do you avoid fear and paralysis and develop the ability to pull the trigger as soon as you see the signal?

Jairek: First, traders need to understand the role that fear can play for them. Fear is nothing more than your nervous system asking if you are prepared. Paralysis is what happens if you aren't prepared, especially with mental rehearsal, and you become overwhelmed.

To illustrate, let's say you're a caveman. As you leave your cave, you see your spear, but you tell yourself, "I'm not going to be gone long. I don't need my spear." As you're out in the jungle, the tree next to you starts shaking and you hear, "R-r-r-o-o-a-a-r-r-r-r!" You're petrified because you are not prepared to defend yourself. Now, consider a second scenario. As you leave the cave, you take your trusty spear with you. This time, when the tree next to you starts to shake and you hear "R-r-r-o-o-a-a-r-r-r-r!" you don't feel scared. You feel excited because you're about to bring home dinner!

The best defense against debilitating fear and paralysis is being prepared—making sure you have the tools and you know how to use them. If you feel fearful the minute you sit down to trade, you're not prepared. Create a checklist of all the daily preparations you need before you trade so that you feel physically, emotionally, and mentally ready to trade. If you have mentally rehearsed and engaged in the other exercises in this discussion; if you understand and embrace your system, have the discipline to follow your rules, and you've done your homework on the long-term trend and the stocks you want to buy; if all of these things are in place, you have no reason to be petrified. Like the caveman in the second scenario, you are about to bring home dinner!

Mark: How can traders keep their confidence after having a series of losses? This can happen to a golfer in a slump or a basketball player who can't hit three pointers. What can they do to get back on track?

Jairek: Just keep following your system. If the system is correct and you are truly following the rules, it's just a matter of time before it gets back on track. You might want to adjust your trading size during this time, but if it's a proven system and you are not deviating from the rules, it will bring you back to profitability. You have to be honest with yourself. Are you really following the system? If you are overriding some part of it, or you only implement some of the rules, then you are not following the system. It can't help you if you don't use it.

Mark: How do you stay positive during the learning curve when you are not yet good enough to produce acceptable results? How do you know it's you and not the system?

Jairek: In all of my experiences, whether someone is an athlete or a psychologist coaching others, or working as a sales rep with a business quota to meet, you are facing what's called a "supervised learning curve." In other words, there is someone looking over your shoulder or giving you feedback from time to time who is helping you spot errors and get better over time. You need an outside perspective to show you what you can't see. If you aren't working with someone, then let your results act as that feedback mechanism. There is no gray here, only black and white. Print your trading results so you can see the reality of your wins and losses.

Mark: How do I know I have the right mentor or coach?

Jairek: That's simple—your results and attitude will improve. The results speak for themselves, if you hire a coach *and* you are following his or her advice consistently. If you are applying 100 percent of your coach's advice and guidance, but your results worsen over a reasonable period of time, then you have the wrong mentor or trainer. It could be the coach's philosophy doesn't work for you. Or the way your coach is presenting doesn't "click." Whatever the reason, you have to find the best match to help you succeed.

Mark: How long do you think people should give themselves to become proficient? Is there a point at which they should give up? Personally, I believe that people should be "unconditionally persistent"—which means they have a commitment to never give up and the confidence to stay the course through thick and thin. What's your opinion?

Jairek: First, you have to decide what you want to achieve and how you are going to become great at it. As we discussed with mastery, we know that there are going to be obstacles and lulls along the way. You must stick with something, learning about yourself and honing your technique, until you achieve mastery. It's a process. Often people underestimate how long mastery takes. With trading, they may underestimate how much is involved—how much science and psychology must come together—so they give up way too soon, because they were not prepared for just how long the learning curve is.

Think about how long doctors must be educated and how diligently they prepare themselves to practice medicine. Do you think that takes only 6 months? Would you go to a doctor who only studied for 6 months? Would you trust the legal advice of an attorney who only went to school for 12 months? In any field, it takes 8 to 10 years to become certified or achieve a doctorate or similar level of mastery. If you are not willing to invest that kind of time, how can you expect to achieve doctoral-degree performance? As the research shows, it takes 10,000 hours of practice to become a master—not 10,000 hours of preparation, but actual practice. So, if that's the starting point, how many hours of trading practice are you willing to commit? To achieve superperformance, it takes a long-term, multiyear, committed endeavor.

Mark: Jairek, thank you so much! I knew this conversation would add an element to this book that takes readers beyond the bare mechanics of trading. Great stuff! Thanks again.

ABOUT THE AUTHOR

Mark Minervini is the author of the best-selling book *Trade Like a Stock Market Wizard: How to Achieve Superperformance in Stocks in Any Market*. Starting with only a few thousand dollars, Mark turned his personal trading account into millions, averaging 220 percent per year for more than five consecutive years with only one losing quarter—an incredible 33,500 percent total return. To put that in perspective, a $100,000 account would explode to more than $30 million in just five years.

To demonstrate the capabilities of his SEPA® trading methodology, in 1997, Mark put up $250,000 of his own money and entered the U.S. Investing Championship. Trading against highly leveraged futures and options traders, Mark traded a long-only stock portfolio to win the real-money investment derby with a 155 percent annual return, a performance that was nearly double the nearest competing money manager.

Mark is featured in *Momentum Masters: A Roundtable Interview with Super Traders* and in Jack Schwager's *Stock Market Wizards: Interviews with America's Top Stock Traders*. Schwager wrote: "Minervini's performance has been nothing short of astounding. Most traders and money managers would be delighted to have Minervini's worst year —a 128 percent gain—as their best."

Mark educates traders about his SEPA® methodology through Minervini Private Access, a streaming communication platform that allows users the unique experience of trading side-by-side with him in real time. He also conducts a live Master Trader Program workshop where he teaches his system in a comprehensive weekend event. You can learn more about Mark at www.minervini.com.

INDEX

ACKNOWLEDGMENTS

First and foremost, I want to acknowledge the two most important people in the world to me: my wife, Elena, and my daughter, Angelia. You inspire me each day to be the best version of myself.

My thanks to Patricia Crisafulli for her valuable input and editing, and to Patricia Wallenburg for once again doing a fabulous job with the book layout. Thank you, Bob Weissman, for working with passion about trading and doing your best to ensure that our clients receive the highest level of service, each and every day.

A special thanks to those who travel from all parts of the world to attend our Master Trader Workshops, to our Minervini Private Access members, and to all my friends on Twitter. I hope this content means as much to you as it has to me throughout my life and career.

To all my friends and family who have supported me over the years, especially my late mother and father—Lea and Nate—without whom nothing would have been possible.

Thank you all.

Better Investing.

Minervini Private Access

A Click Away

www.minervini.com

EARN WHILE YOU LEARN

Trade with Mark Minervini – LIVE!

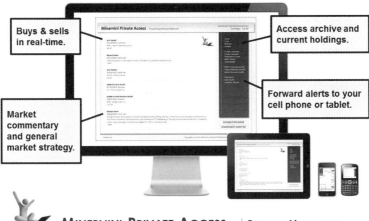

Buys & sells in real-time.

Access archive and current holdings.

Forward alerts to your cell phone or tablet.

Market commentary and general market strategy.

MINERVINI PRIVATE ACCESS™ | PREMIUM MEMBERSHIP

✅ **Real-Time Platform** allows you to trade side-by-side with Mark Minervini and receive his up to the minute buys & sells as they happen right on your PC, cell phone or tablet.

✅ **Interactive Training Room** is where Mark reviews trades, conducts educational study sessions and answers your questions while you view his trading desktop LIVE!

✅ **TradingLogger**™ Gives you the tools to track, analyze and perfect your trading with proprietary analytics. Take control and know the truth about your trading.

> "Most traders would be delighted to have Minervini's worst year – a 128 percent gain – as their best."
>
> **Jack Schwager**
> **Stock Market Wizards**

> "One of the most highly-respected independent traders of our generation."
>
> **Charles Kirk**
> **The Kirk Report**

To learn more go to: **www.minervini.com**

Other Books by Mark Minervini

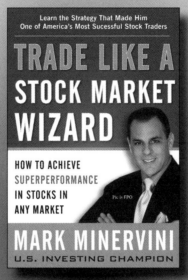

Learn the Strategy That Made Him
One of America's Most Sucessful Stock Traders

TRADE LIKE A
STOCK MARKET
WIZARD

HOW TO ACHIEVE
SUPERPERFORMANCE
IN STOCKS IN
ANY MARKET

Pic is FPO

MARK MINERVINI
U.S. INVESTING CHAMPION

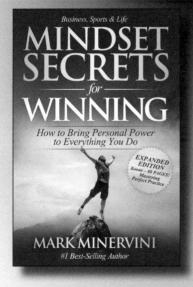

Business, Sports & Life

MINDSET
SECRETS
for
WINNING

*How to Bring Personal Power
to Everything You Do*

EXPANDED
EDITION
Bonus – 80 PAGES!
Mastering
Perfect Practice

MARK MINERVINI
#1 Best-Selling Author

A Roundtable Interview with Super Traders

MOMENTUM
MASTERS

Mark Minervini, David Ryan,
Dan Zanger and Mark Ritchie II